THE […]

OF

LIP-READING *for* THE DEAF

(BRUHN LIP-READING SYSTEM)

MARTHA E. BRUHN

PRINCIPAL OF THE MÜLLER-WALLE
SCHOOL OF LIP-READING AND THE
MÜLLER-WALLE TRAINING SCHOOL
FOR TEACHERS IN BOSTON, MASS.

1920
PRESS OF THOS. P. NICHOLS & SON CO.
LYNN, MASS.

CONTENTS

PART ONE

PART TWO

PART THREE

PREFACE

THIS book is the Third Revised Edition of the Müller-Walle Method of Lip Reading for the Deaf.

It contains a series of thirty lessons, including exercises, sentence practice and story studies in exercise form, and is intended for the use of those who have become deaf after having acquired a full knowledge of speech, as well as for use in schools for deaf children. This includes high school and college students whose hearing has become impaired before their education has been completed; adults whose hearing is more or less defective; and children in the elementary schools for the deaf who have previously received a certain amount of instruction in speech-reading.

The following are a few suggestions for the teacher: —

FIRST

This book is intended for both teacher and pupil, to be used as a text-book in learning the principal movements in each group of sounds, and as a guide book for self-instruction at home.

It is not a book of instruction showing *how* lip-reading should be taught, as the difficulty, or rather, the impossibility of such a task is very evident, since movement, the very foundation of speech, cannot be described in words or pictures, but must be shown to the student by an able teacher who is well acquainted with the physiology of speech.

It is comparatively easy to describe the position of each individual organ of speech when a single sound is produced; a little more difficult to describe the transition from one position to another; but it is well-nigh impossible through mere description to present the mingling of a series of incessant outward, inward, downward, forward and backward movements, all united for the time into one great whole.

Such processes can never be accurately described, they must be shown, — acted out, so to speak. Therefore, the method of conducting the rapid syllable drills that should accompany each lesson can only be shown by the trained teacher and is here omitted. Incorrect use of such drills does more harm than good.

Let the pupil fix the principal movements of each group in his mind by constant repetition of the mirror exercises given in each lesson.

SECOND

The sentences under B in each lesson are to be used for home practice. They should never be practiced with the mirror. Teachers should urge pupils to interest one or more members of the family or some friends to repeat the sentences to them. *The more lips the student has to read the, better.* Encourage pupils to practice among themselves.

THIRD

Do not have the pupils commit rules to memory. For example, "**fä** — lower lip against upper teeth and downward movement of jaw." It should be recognized as such, but it is not necessary to test the pupil's knowledge by asking him to define the movements. The rapid comprehension of such movements does not depend so much upon any actual knowledge as upon skill and ability. This ability is attained, not through long conscientious memorizing of difficult rules, but by the application of the fundamentals of those rules by continuous practice under proper guidance.

This proper guidance in the art of lip-reading is much the same as in athletics. The athlete and the lip-reader acquire most of their knowledge by observing and imitating the movements of their teachers and those about them.

BOSTON, MASS., *September, 1919.*

PART ONE

CHAPTER I

Origin of the Instruction of Lip-Reading

THE art of lip-reading is not new. Many hundred years ago the attempt was made to teach speech to the congenitally deaf, and also the art of reading speech from the lips. The credit of the first successful teaching belongs to the Spanish Benedictine Monk, Pietro Ponce, who died in 1588.

Almost contemporaneously there appeared in other countries similar attempts which were more or less successful. In England, it was the famous and learned Bishop Wallis, and in Holland, the Swiss physician, Ammann, who first introduced the oral method into these countries. But, unfortunately, the results were meagre owing to the lack of good institutions.

The method became somewhat better known when a German named Samuel Heinecke, a teacher in Eppendorf, near Hamburg, opened a school in Leipzig in 1787. But he so closely guarded the method as a secret, that his work was retarded in its progress after his death. In France, on the other hand, the Abbé de l'Epée introduced an oral method and sign language which is still in use there and which spread into Germany as well as into other countries. However, the work begun by Heinecke also progressed. The advantages of the German method were recognized more and more, and finally this was the method used not only in Germany but also in other countries.

And, now year after year, thousands of pupils leave such schools equipped with the blessings of the oral method, and with the art of leading speech from the lips, which formerly seemed out of the question for children who were born deaf.

CHAPTER II

I. The deaf may be divided into two classes:

I. Those who, being born deaf, must be taught to speak as well as to read the lips.

II. Those who, having lost their hearing after acquiring speech, need only to learn to read the lips.

The instruction necessary for both Classes I and II may be divided as follows:

1. The study of the visible characteristics of the *positions* of the organs of speech in producing a *single* sound.

2. The study of the visible characteristics of the organs of speech in *the passing from one sound to another*.

To those who are born deaf, both of these kinds of study are equally important, but for the hard-of-hearing adult by far greater stress is laid on the second kind, namely, — *movements*, and this is the basis of the Müller-Walle Method.

What are *movements?* They are the passing from one position to another, or from one sound to another, which cannot be done without a so-called *inter-movement*.

For example, get the mouth in a position to produce the sound **ä**. Then change the position to produce **ōō**. You will notice that in order to combine these sounds **ä‿ōō**, there is an *upward* inter-movement. Now get the mouth into the position for the sound **ōō**. Change that position to **ä**. The inter-movement is now a *backward* movement, **ōō‿ä**. Thus, varying the order has changed the inter-movement. This shows that every sound must not only be studied alone (which is very easy for the deaf adult) but also in ever-varying combinations. Conversation which he wishes to follow is the passing from one sound to another. The number of combinations is, of course, as boundless as the conversation itself and can never be exhausted, but, on the other hand, by studying the characteristics of these inter-movements we find that they may be classified in a clear, orderly way, easy for the pupil to grasp, and logically arranged for the use of the teacher.

This book contains the study of these visible characteristics of the movements of the organs of speech, graded to suit the ability of the average pupil, and so arranged that when he has completed the lessons outlined herein, he will have the same knowledge of lip-reading that the student of music has acquired when he knows his scales, keys, exercises, etc. And, just as the latter has at the same time been led to appreciate and understand and read music, so the former has been led to apply his knowledge gained by drills and exercises to the reading of general conversation. A good pianist must also be a correct interpreter of the composer — a good lip-reader must also be a quick observer, and acquire the ability to make the *eye* do the work of the *ear*.

To become proficient in the art of lip-reading requires patience and perseverance, but the time is short compared to that spent in music.

II. The outlines of the lessons in this book can be used to better advantage if a few simple suggestions are followed by both pupil and teacher.

In the first place, the teacher should be in a position to allow the light to fall on his face. The earlier the lip-reader learns to choose a favorable position when trying to follow conversation the better for him. Later, at home and in company, having once acquired the habit, he can, without much disturbance to those about him, place himself in the correct position. It is good practice for the teacher to change his position by standing up and moving about, thus training the eye to become accustomed to these changes.

Of equal importance to the position in which the lip-reader must learn to place himself, is the habit he must form of studying the facial expression and attitude of the speaker. It is astonishing how much one may learn by observing the changes of expression which constantly pass over the features of the speaker. Take the simple word "Oh!" How easily one detects even without understanding any part of the conversation whether it is an expression of joy, of sorrow, of pain, or of surprise. The emotions are almost always accompanied by gestures of the hands, head, or shoulders, and sometimes all these combined, and they form an important part in the conversation which the lip-reader must observe as carefully as he does the lips.

Another important fact that must be firmly fixed in the mind of the student as soon as he begins to read general conversation is that he must not concentrate his thought on the individual word, but must try to grasp the meaning of the sentence as a whole. Just as the eye is trained to take in at a glance a sentence of fifty or more letters in reading type, so, also, must it be trained in reading speech to combine rapid movements of the lips, and think of them as one united group.

The student who becomes easily confused because he does not "see" every movement will require a much longer time to master the art than one who, as we say, "can put two and two together" and let his *mind* supply what his *eye* has missed.

But, on the other hand, it is only through a conscientious and thorough study of the syllable drills and exercises which form the foundation of the art of lip-reading that the mind and the eye *are* thus trained to work together.

For this reason much emphasis is laid in this method on drill work to lighten the task later on.

A person cannot read music rapidly and intelligently without a good foundation. Likewise, a person cannot read the lips well without a clear understanding of the characteristics of the movements.

In music, also, one must be able to grasp the composer's phrasing as a whole; in lip-reading one must be able to grasp the sentence as a whole.

The purpose of this book is, in brief, to provide the student and teacher with sufficient material for the thorough mastering of the study of the movements of the lips in drill form, and to suggest, by means of its exercises and short stories, the wide range of material for conversational practice.

CHAPTER III

HOW TO PRACTICE THE EXERCISE

A pupil should, while learning, have the sentences given by his teacher repeated by as many different people as possible. It is important that the speaker should speak distinctly, yet avoid all exaggerations. Speaking in a loud voice, or with the head lowered, or emphasizing each word with a gesture of the head must be avoided.

Whoever undertakes the task of practicing with a pupil, should understand clearly the aim of all practice. This is principally to train the eye to perceive, distinguish and combine the outward movements of the organs of speech, not, however, to give the pupil a large number of new subjects. In practicing, it is neither the quantity nor the nature of the subject, but the correct arrangement that must be considered first and foremost.

A subject for instruction is correctly arranged when it starts with the simple and gradually leads up to the more difficult. For a lip-reader a word is "simple" when the movement is plainly visible; "difficult," on the contrary, when he must recognize it by insignificant characteristics. Thus, for example, a monosyllable may be much more difficult to see than a word of many syllables, because the latter is made up of different movements and contrasts are seen more readily. Only those who are well acquainted with the physiology of speech can judge between the simple and the difficult. It is, therefore, necessary for the teacher to make a study of the same. Before beginning the instruction, he should study the movements carefully before a mirror, according to the directions in the text-book. He must know thoroughly each exercise in order to be able to show the same correctly. It is, however, not at all necessary to treat each given exercise the same with all pupils. Each must be adapted to the ability of the latter. But one rule holds true for all, namely: *Repeat constantly the exercises already learned by using the same words over again in different connections.* Change a sentence from the interrogative to the positive, from the affirmative to the negative. Avoid practicing a list of words or names by themselves. Aside from the fact that it would be impossible to go over all the words in the language, the memorizing of names is of little value. If the pupil is to learn certain names which occur frequently, let them be put into sentences and accustom him gradually to see the whole picture. Whoever learns to read sentences well, will seldom fail when one contains a name or word not practiced before.

The first few lessons should not be too long, as the eyes and nerves will become fatigued; frequent pauses should be made to rest the eyes. The speaker should speak perfectly naturally, neither too loudly nor too softly, since in either case the face assumes a changed expression. But above all things he must not exaggerate the movements or try to *over*-articulate. If he naturally speaks very rapidly, he may, in giving the pupil a new lesson, try it a little slower, but never without repeating the same in his natural way. This is very important since otherwise the pupil will never be able to follow him in general conversation.

If a mistake is made in recognizing a word or syllable, the same should be written down and shown to the pupil. Then, by placing the correct word with the mistaken one, the difference may be shown. There are many words which look alike when pronounced by themselves, but these are rarely mistaken in a sentence where the meaning helps to distinguish the same. Although sentences, stories and general conversation are to be practiced, yet a systematic drill of well-arranged syllables by an experienced teacher is necessary to train the eye to distinguish the most insignificant movements of the lips which are necessary in order to follow long and difficult sentences.

The aim of this chapter has been to show the pupil how to practice, since much of his success depends upon the good will and patience of his family and friends.

PART TWO

Note. Each lesson is divided into three parts: —

A. Study and mirror practice.

B. Sentence practice and vocabulary.

C. Stories. (Omitted in Lessons I, II and III.)

LESSON I

A

I. The difference between the **position** and the **movement** of the mouth: —

In the *position*, we have one single sound prolonged.

In the *movement*, we have the passing from one sound to another.

(**a**) Four principal movements: —

Lower jaw moves upwards and downwards.
Lips move forward and backward.

ä ō o͞o ā ē

II. Class I of Consonants.

(Subdivided into three parts.)

Mouth closed:
1. **f, v,** . . .lower lip against upper teeth.
2. **s, z,** soft **c,** . . .teeth together.
3. **m, b, p,** . . .lips closed.

th is formed by placing the tongue between the teeth.

For **sh** the lips assume a somewhat square appearance.

w and **wh** have the same forward movement as **o͞o.**

III. Syllables formed by prefixing consonants of Class I to vowels under **I.**

fä	**fō**	**fōō**	**fā**	**fēē**
sä	**sō**	**sōō**	**sā**	**sēē**
mä	**mō**	**mōō**	**mā**	**mēē**
. . .	**thō**	. . . .	**thā**	**thē**
shä	**shō**	**shōō**	**shā**	**shē**

Note. Only such syllables are given throughout the thirty lessons as occur in real words.

IV. Mirror practice on sounds.

1. Difference between **ä** (far) and **ōō** (food).

Pronounce rapidly in one breath: —

fäfäfä — **fōō** (prolong the **ōō** somewhat)

Notice in pronouncing **ōō** the lips move forward, while in **ä** we see a downward movement of the jaw.

2. Difference between **m** and **f.**

Pronounce rapidly in one breath: —

fä**f**ä**f**ä — **m**ä**m**ä**m**ä

Notice that in **f** the upper teeth are visible, while in **m** the lips are closed.

3. Difference between **s** and **m.**

Pronounce **s**ä**s**ä**s**ä — **s**ēē; then **m**ä**m**ä**m**ä — **m**ēē.

Notice that both upper and lower teeth are visible in pronouncing **s,** while in **m,** the lips are closed.

4. Difference between **ä** (far) and **ā** (face).

Pronounce **fäfäfä** — **fā** in one breath.

Notice that in **ä** the jaw drops, while in **ā**, we see a slight backward movement of the lips.

Notice the same in **mämämä** — **mā** and **säsäsä** — **sā**.

5. Difference between **ā** (face) and **ē** (feet).

Pronounce **fāfāfā** — **fē** in one breath.
Pronounce **māmāmā** — **mē** in one breath.
Pronounce **sāsāsā** — **sē** in one breath.

Notice that in **ē** the lips are drawn back more than in **ā**.

6. Difference between **ō** (go) and **ōō** (food).

Pronounce **fōfōfō** — **fōō** in one breath.
Pronounce **mōmōmō** — **mōō** in one breath.
Pronounce **sōsōsō** — **sōō** in one breath.

Notice that in both **ō** and **ōō** the lips move forward, — more forward in **ōō** than **ō**.

7. Syllables under III should be practised in groups of two and three until pupil is perfectly familiar with the movements.

8. How a syllable drill may be used to lead up to a sentence.

shē	**mā**
shē	**fā**
shē	**fō**
shē	**mä**
shē	**mōō**
shē	**sōō**

thā	**sō**		
thā	**mā**	**sō**	
thā	**mā**	**sā**	**sō**
thā	**mā**	**sē**	**mē**

They may see me sew the seam.

9. Difference between **what** and **where.**

Notice that **what** has a forward and downward movement; **where** has a forward and backward movement.

what is?
where is?

what was?
where was?

B

I. Sentence Practice.

(a) She may.
They may.
You may.
We may.
May we?
May she?
May you?
May they?

May they pay?
May they show?
May they move?
May they sew?
May they see?
May they say?
May she say?
May she pay?

They say so to me.
They may say so.
They may say so to you.
She may say so to you.
She may sew for you.
She may sew for me.

May we show them the way?
May we see the show?
May we pay for the palm?
May we move to the farm?
May we sew for them?

(b) Where is the farm?
Where is the foam?
Where is the palm? psalm? ship? shop?
Where is the vase? wave? soap? soup?
Where is the sofa? beef? shoe? show?

What is on the sofa?
What is on the ship?
What is on the farm?
What is on the wave?
What is in the shoe?
What is in the soup?
What is in the vase?

Show me the way.
Show me the farm. palm. psalm.
Show me the soup. soap. beef.

(c) She may show me the way to the farm.
They say they may move.
They seem to be far away.
They seem to be so far away.
They seem to be in the way.

Though they seem to be far away,....
You may see them.
You may see them on the farm.
You may see the foam.
You may see them on the ship.
You may see them on the way to the ship.
You may see the ship in the bay.

They seem to be sharp.
They seem to be safe.
They say the ship is safe.
They say the ship is safe in the bay.
They may be on the way to the shoe shop.
They may see me at the farm.
They may seem to be sharp.

(d) The same ship is in the bay.
Show me both the soap and the soup.
What is the shape of the vase?
You may weigh the beef for me.
We may move to the farm.
She may show me the shape of the shoe.
We may bathe in the sea.
They both seem to be so far away.
She was on the way to the ship.
Pay for the beef at the shop.
They show faith in you.
They may be on the same ship with you.
Was the ship far away?
Was she on the way to the farm?
Who was in the shop with you?

II. Vocabulary.

These words may be used to form new sentences:

NOUNS AND PRONOUNS — farm, foam, fame, ship, shop, shoe, face, faith, foe, fee, sea, soap, soup, Sue, salve, sheep, show, shape, zoo, May, bay, bow, booth, beef, seam, bee, beam, path, bath, wave, waif, shame.

VERBS — sew, pay, may, say, see, be, seem, pass, bathe, move, mow, wave, weave, cease, sieze, was.

ADJECTIVES AND ADVERBS — far, away, same, where, sharp.

LESSON II

I. Diphthongs.

öû (as in föûnd) or **öŵ** (as in töŵn). These sounds are composed of **ä** and **ōō**. Pronounce **ä‿ōō** rapidly and you have the sound **öû**.

ī (as in fīnd). This sound is composed of **ä** and **ē**. Pronounce **ä‿ē** rapidly and you have the sound **ī**.

öĭ (as in öĭl) or **öy̆** (as in böy̆). These sounds are composed of **âw** and **ē**. Pronounce **âw‿ē** rapidly and you have **öĭ**.

II. Mirror Practice on Sounds.

1. Difference between **öû** and **ī**.

Pronounce rapidly in one breath: —

öûöûöû — ī

möûmöûmöû — mī

Notice the downward and forward movement in **öû** and the downward and backward movement of **ī**.

2. Difference between **ī** and **öĭ**.

Pronounce rapidly in one breath: —

fīfīfī — föĭ

sīsīsī — söĭ

Notice the downward and backward movement in **ī** and the forward and backward movement in **öĭ**.

3. Difference between **öû** and **öĭ**.

Pronounce rapidly in one breath: —

öûöûöû — öĭ

möûmöûmöû — möĭ

Notice the downward and forward movement in **öû** and the forward and backward movement in **öĭ**.

4. Syllable drill leading up to sentences.

mā	**sē**	
mā	**sä**	
mā	**soi**	
mā	**foi**	
mā	**mou**	
mā	**fou**	
mä	**fou**	
mä	**fi**	
sō	**fi**	
sō	**fä**	
sō	**fä**	**sou**

So far south.

They are so far south.

They may be so far south.

B

I. Sentence Practice.

NOTE. Although the Consonant "l" does not belong in Class 1 of Consonants, the auxiliaries *shall* and *will* are introduced here. For "l", we see the action of the tongue as the tip is raised.

(a)

I shall.	You shall.	They shall see.
I will.	They shall.	They will be.
I may.	They may.	You will be.
You may.	You may be.	You shall be.
You will.	They shall be.	You shall see.

What shall I see? buy?
What shall I pay? say?
What shall I move?
You may move. pay. buy.
May we show them the way?

May we see the show?
May we buy the soup?
May we buy the soap?
May we pay for the palm?
May we say so to them?
May we move to the farm?

(b) I shall bow.
I shall bow to them. to you. to both of them.
She will bow to me. to you. to them.
Will she bow?
Will she bow to them?
Will they bow?
Will they bow to my wife?
The boy will bow to my wife.
I shall bow to them.
I shall bow to them on the ship.
How shall I bow?
Show me how to bow.
Where is the boy? the pipe? the fife?
Where is the pie? the scythe? the mouse?
Where was the mouse?
Where was my wife? my fife? my pipe?
Show me the pipe.
Show me both the pipe and the fife.
I shall buy both the pipe and the fife.
I shall buy both the pipe and the fife for the boy.

(c) Where will the boy be?
Where shall I see the boy?
Where shall you buy the pie?
What will you buy for me?
What will you buy for my wife?
What will you buy for the boy?
How will you sew the seam?
How will you bow to them?
How will you show me the way?
How will you pay for the farm?
Where was the boy?

The boy is in the South.
The boy will buy the farm.
I shall buy the sofa at the same shop.
They shall buy the shoes for the boy.
What size is the shoe?
The shoe is the same size.
I will buy the same size for you.
I will show you the palm by and by.
We may pass the shop on the way.
She will show me how to weave.
She will show me how to sew.
I may buy the shoes at the same shop.
I may buy both of them.
We will pay for both of them.

(d) They say they may buy the farm.
I will buy five pies at the shop for you.
Pay for the shoes on the way to the farm.
The boy found the palm in the South.
My wife will buy the shoes for the boy.
Shall I show you how to weave?
Shall I buy the scythe if it is sharp?
By the way, will you show me the shoes?
They may wish to see them.
Save the pie for the boy.
Why shall I save them?
We found the vase in the shop.
I may buy them for my wife.
We may buy the scythe for the boy on the farm.
The boy found the mouse in the shoe.

II. Vocabulary.

Use these words to form new sentences:

NOUNS AND PRONOUNS — boy, bow, bar, mouth, south, wife, fife, pipe, pie, scythe, size, sight, I, my, thy.

VERBS — buy, shall, will, bow.

ADJECTIVES AND ADVERBS — how, shy, why.

LESSON III

A

I. Class II of Consonants.

(Sub-divided into two parts.)

Mouth open { **1.** **k,** hard **g,** hard **c, d, t.**
2. **h, l, n, r** (initial in word or syllable).

The first five, namely, **k, g, c, d** and **t,** are what we call explosive sounds.

The last four, namely, **h, l, n** and **r,** are the long or duration sounds.

In this lesson we practice only **k,** hard **g** and hard **c** before a vowel and mostly words of one syllable.

In pronouncing these letters before a vowel, the mouth is open, — the degree of opening depending upon the vowel that follows.

The externally visible characteristics of these letters are the cheek and jaw movement.

II. Mirror Practice on Sounds.

1. Syllables formed by prefixing consonants already learned to vowels.

fä	**fō**	**fā**	**fōō**	**fēē**	**fī**	**föû**	**föĭ**
sä	**sō**	**sā**	**sōō**	**sēē**	**sī**	**söû**	**söĭ**
mä	**mō**	**mā**	**mōō**	**mēē**	**mī**	**möû**	**möĭ**
cä	**cō**	**cā**	**cōō**	**kēē**	**kī**	**cöw**	**cöĭ**

Notice in each group of syllables that letters that look alike are not used in the same group; for example, **m, b, p,** or **f, v,** or **k, g, c.** They are not distinguishable and one of each group has been selected to represent it. Never try to see any difference between **co** and **go**, or **ki** and **guy**. If **co** is practiced later in a sentence like "Will you **go** with me?" it will be correctly read. Occasionally a sentence like "Will you **b**ake a cake?" might be mistaken for "Will you **m**ake a cake?" but this error is too slight to deserve any notice here.

2. Pronounce rapidly in one breath: —

fä**f**ä**f**ä — **k**ä
sä**s**ä**s**ä — **k**ä
mä**m**ä**m**ä — **k**ä

Compare these visible characteristics: —

f mouth closed by placing lower lip against upper teeth.
s mouth closed by placing teeth together.
m mouth closed by placing lips together.
k mouth open.

3. Syllable drill leading up to a sentence.

sō	**fē**	
sō	**fä**	
sō	**cō**	
fä	**cō**	
mi	**cō**	
thā	**kē**	
thā	**mā**	**kē**
mā	**thā**	**kē**
mā	**shē**	**kē**

May she keep the comb?

4. Further comparison in the following sentences.

Where is the **c**omb?
Where is the **f**oam?

Where is the **c**ase?
Where is the **v**ase?

Where is the **k**ey?
Where is the **s**ea?

Where is the **c**ar?
Where is the **sh**ah?

5. Pronounce

Do you
Did you

Notice that in pronouncing "**Do** you," we have only one forward movement, since in rapid conversation the two words are not separated. In "**Did** you," we have two distinct movements, — a backward and a forward movement.

B

I. Sentence Practice.

(a) They go.
They may go.
They shall go.
We shall go.

We may go.
We may go away.
We may go with them.
We may go away with them.

Did you go?
Did you go with them?
How far did you go?
How far will you go?
How far did they go with you?

May I go?
May I go with you?
May I go on the car with you?
Shall I go on the car with them?

Go with me.
Go with them.
Go with them if you wish.
Go South with them.
She may go South with me.

(b) Can you come?
Can you go?
Can you carve?
Can you see?
Can you pay?

Can you give them away?
Can you pay for them?
Can you see so far?
Can you show me how?
Can you keep them?
Do you keep a cow?
Do you show them how?
Where do you see the car?
How do you pay for them?
Why do you give him the coffee?
Where do you see the ship?
How do you carve the beef?
Why do they go so far South?
Where do they come from?
Where did they come from?
Why do you go to the cave with them?
Why did you give them the key?
Why did they go to the same farm?
Where did you keep the key?
Where did you go for the palm?
Where did you see the comb?

(c) I will give it to you.
I may give it to them.
We will give it to them.
We may give it up.
Shall we give it up?
Shall we give it away?
May I give it to you?
May I give you the key?
May I give you the case?

Give it to me.
Give it away.
Give it to him when he comes.
Give it to them.
Give me some advice.
You may give it to me.
Will you give it to me?

Will you keep it?
Will you come?
Will you go?
When will you go?
When will you come?
When will you give it to me?
Give it to me when you come.
Give it to the boy.
Give it to my wife.

(d) Will you give me a cup of coffee?
I will give you a cup of cocoa.
May I give you a piece of cake?
My wife gave the boy a piece of cake.

How is the coffee?
Have you found the key?
Where does this car go?
Does this car go to the Cape?
I must get the car.
You must not give up.
May I buy the comb in that shop?
I shall go to the game with the boy.
When the boy came, I gave him the cake.

Will you show me the way to the cove?
The coffee was in the cup.
The comb was in the case.
When he comes, I shall ask him to give you the key for the case.
How much did you say that you would pay for the comb and the case?
Did you say that you would buy the same kind of shoes?
How much did you say that you would pay for the shoes that you will buy for the boy on the farm?

II. Vocabulary.

These words may be used to form new sentences:

NOUNS AND PRONOUNS — cake, calf, cape, car, cargo, carp, case, cave, cocoa, coffee, coke, comb, cook, couch, cow, cube, cuckoo, key, kindness, game.

VERBS — carve, keep, came, come, go, gave.

ADJECTIVES — calm, cool, kind, gay.

LESSON IV

A

I. Vowel Sounds — **ër** (her) **ïr** (fir) **ür** (fur), and **â** (fall).

II, Mirror Practice on Sounds.

1. Difference between **ō** (old) and **ër** (ir or ur).

Pronounce rapidly in one breath: —

fōfōfō — fïr
mōmōmō — mïr
sōsōsō — sïr

Notice in pronouncing **ō** we have a forward movement of both lips, while in **ïr** (**ër** or **ür**) the lower lip moves further forward than the upper.

2. Difference between **ä** (far) and **â** (fall).

Pronounce rapidly in one breath: —

fäfäfä — fâ
mämämä — mâ
säsäsä — sâ

Notice that **ä** has a downward movement of the jaw. **â** is not so far downward as **ä** and not so far forward as **ō.**

3. Difference between prefixes **rē** and **bē.**

Pronounce rapidly in one breath: —

rērērē — bē
rēcei — **rē**cei — **rē**cei — **bē**see

Notice that **rē** has a forward and backward movement. **bē** has lips closed, and then a backward movement (like **mē**).

4. Syllable drills leading to sentences.

sä	**mē**	
sä	**sē**	
sä	**kē**	
sō	**kē**	
sō	**ki**	
sō	**mi**	
mi	**fir**	
mi	**fâ**	
mi	**ser**	
rē	**ser**	**reserve**

Reserve them for me.

rē	**mō**	
rē	**sē**	
rē	**mā**	
rē	**câ**	
rē	**fer**	
rē	**ser**	
rē	**lē**	
bē	**lē**	
bē	**cā**	**became**

What became of her?

B

I. Sentence Practice.

(a)

I believe.	I remain.
I receive.	I recall.
I remember.	I remove.
I remark.	I refuse.

Because I refuse.
Because I remember.
Did you remember?
Did you remain?
Shall you remain?

Shall you refuse?
Did you receive?
What did you receive?

Did you receive my letter?
Do you believe she received the letter?
Do you believe she received the report?
Do you believe she will receive them?
How did you receive it?
Where did you receive it?
Where did you say that you received it?
Who received it?

I believe they will receive it.
I believe they will receive it to-morrow.
Did he receive you?
Do you remember?
You must remember.
You must remember what I say.
Remember me to them.
Do you remember them?
Do you remember where they came from?
Do you remember the way?
Do you remember the remark?
I believe I remember the remark.
I believe they will refuse to remain.
I believe they will remember me.
Remember to give me the report.
Shall I report the remark?
Shall I show you the report?
Shall I remain?

Do you believe that she will report the remark?
He may refuse to go.
He may refuse to pay for it.
I believe she will refuse to resign.
Why did you resign?
You may refer to me.
To whom do you refer?

I refer to her.
She may refer to the remark?
Do you believe that she refers to him?

(c) I shall remain.
I shall remain with them.
They may wish to remain on the farm.
Who will remain with you?
Why do you wish to remain on the ship?
They say they will remain.
What became of them?
What became of the boy?
What became of the boy we saw on the farm?

Do you remember what became of them?
Remove the key.
I shall remove the key.
She removed her cape.
She removed her cape when she came in.
Remind me to show it to you.
Remind me to show you the report.
Remind me to show you the case.
Remind me to show you the palm.
Remind me to show you my furs.
Remind me to go.
Remind them to come.
Remind them to go to the game.
Remind me to buy the cake.

(d) Remember me to your mother.
Remember to buy some cocoa on the way.
We must remember to give them the key to the case.
You must remember to make a report.
Shall I remove the key from the case?
The remark was reported to me.
I do not wish to repeat the remark.
Did you receive my letter before you came?
I received five letters this morning.
I believe they will remain on the farm.
When you go to the shop, remember to buy some coffee.

I saw them on the way.
I remember that I saw the boy on the ship.
Can you remember the size of the case?
Can you remember the shape?
Did the boy say that he refused to resume the work on the farm?
I shall refuse to pay for them.
I refuse to say anything about it.
Why did she refuse to bow to you?
Did you buy the *Review of Reviews* on the way?
Will you remind me to buy the *Review of Reviews?*
If they do not remember we must remind them.
Remind me to show you the report before you go.
You may reserve five of them for me.

II. Vocabulary.

Use these words to form new sentences:

NOUNS — firm, fir, fur, sir, curve, shawl, thaw, remark, surf, serf.

VERBS — serve, receive, remove, remain, resume, rely, refer, remember, reserve, became, begin, began.

ADJECTIVES OR ADVERBS — firm, before, below.

Explanatory Note on Exercise Stories.

Most teachers have the pupils read over stories before they are told to them. I have found that by so doing the pupils lost the real interest in the stories.

By arranging them in exercise form I have tried to make them serve a two-fold purpose: — first, to supplement the subject matter with many every-day conversational phrases which should be familiar to the pupil and, second, to let the pupil feel that he is being led up to a climax or point of a story in a conversational way, and thus hold his interest to the end.

One story suggests "shopping," another "theatre," another "traveling," etc., all of which make useful subjects for conversation.

After the exercise has been practised, the whole story (given at the end of each lesson) should be read from beginning to end without interruption. It would be well to review the other stories already studied from time to time by telling them in one's own words, without repetition.

At the end of the thirty lessons, the pupil ought to be ready to read simple stories from the lips without having them arranged in exercise form.

It is well at all times for the teacher to keep in mind the suggestion already given in Chapter III that *it is not the quantity, nor the nature of the subject, but the correct arrangement that must be considered first and foremost.*

C — Exercise Story

I am thirsty.
I am hungry.
She was hungry.
She was hungry when she came home.
They were hungry when they returned home.
Please give me something to eat.
Please give me a glass of water.
I should like a drink of cold water for I am very thirsty.
"Oh, I am so thirsty," said the crow one day.
"Where can I get some water?"
There is some water in that vase.
There must be some water in the vase.
There was not much water in the vase.
The crow tried to get the water.
The crow put his bill into the vase.
The crow put his bill into the vase as far as he could reach.
But the water was too low.
He said to himself, ...
He said to himself, "I must have that water."
"How can I get it?"
"I must think it over."

Have you thought how you can get the water?
What would you do?
What would you do in my place?
What would you have done in the crow's place?

Have you thought of a way?
Do you think you can find a way?
Did the crow find a way?
Is the crow a wise bird?
Does the crow know how to think?

The crow though a moment.
The crow thought a moment and then said to himself, . . .
He said to himself, ...
He said to himself, "I know what I will do."
"I will drop these pebbles into the water."
"I will drop these pebbles into the vase."
They will sink to the bottom.
That will make the water rise.
That will make the water rise so that I can reach it.
So the wise old crow went to work.
He said to himself, "Where there's a will, there's a way."

THE THIRSTY CROW

"Oh, I am so thirsty," cried an old black crow. "Ah, there is a vase of water. Now I will have a drink."

So the crow flew down to the vase. There was some water in the vase, but not very much. The crow put his bill in as far as he could reach, but the water was so low he could not reach it.

He said to himself, "I must have that water," and he sat down to think it over. A crow is a very wise bird. A crow knows how to think. Finally he said, "I know what I will do. I will drop these pebbles into the vase. They will sink to the bottom, and that will make the water rise in the vase so that I can reach it."

So the wise old crow went to work. He said to himself, "Where there's a will, there's a way."

LESSON V

A

I. h — before a vowel.

h has no movement of its own, but prolongs the vowel sound that follows it.

hä (like **ä** prolonged)
hō (like **ō** prolonged)
hōō (like **ōō** prolonged)

hä, hō, hōō, hā, hē, höû, hī, höĭ, hër, hâ

II. Mirror Practice: —

Note. Remember that **h** belongs to Class **II** of consonants. (See Lesson **III.**)

1. Difference between **h** and **m.**

Repeat rapidly in one breath: —

the **h**öû the **h**öû the **h**öû — the **m**öû

Notice that in **h**öû the mouth remains open, while in **m**öû the lips are brought together.

Practice:

the **house,** the **house,** the **house** — the **mouse.**
Where is the **house?** Where is the **mouse?**

2. Difference between **h** and **f.**

Repeat rapidly in one breath: —

the **h**oe the **h**oe the **h**oe — the **f**oe

Notice that in **h**ō the mouth remains open, while in **f**ō it is closed by placing the lower lip against the upper teeth.

3. Difference between **h** and **s.**

Repeat rapidly in one breath: —

the **hē** the **hē** the **hē** — the **sē**

Notice that in **hē** the mouth remains open, while in **sē** it is closed by bringing the teeth together.

4. Difference between **h** and hard **c.**

Repeat rapidly in one breath: —

the **hâ** the **hâ** the **hâ** — the **câ**

Notice that in both **hâ** and **câ** the mouth remains open. In **hâ** the sound is prolonged, while in **câ** the breath is expelled forcibly, so that we see more cheek and jaw movement.

5. Further comparison in the following words: —

the **h**arp — the **c**arp
the **h**oop — the **c**oop
the **h**ole — the **c**oal
the **h**ome — the **c**omb

(See note under 4.)

6. Syllable drill leading up to a sentence.

hē	**mā**			
hē	**mā**	**sā**		
hē	**sâ**			
hē	**sâ**	**mē**		
hē	**sâ**	**her**		
sō	**hē**			
sō	**hē**	**mā**		
sō	**hē**	**mā**	**fâ**	
sō	**hē**	**mā**	**sē**	
sō	**hē**	**mā**	**shō**	
sō	**hē**	**mā**	**sā**	**sō**
sō	**hē**	**mā**	**sē**	**her**
hē	**sâ**	**her**		

I believe he saw her in the hall.

B

I. Sentence Practice.

(a)

Have you?	Whose horse have they?
Have they?	Whose harp have we?
Have we?	Whose house have you?
Have I?	Whose hoe have I?
How have I?	
What have I?	I hope so.
Where have I?	I hope to hear from you.
Where have we?	I hope that he will go.
Where have they?	
Where have you?	We hope to see them.
What have you?	We hope to see him.
	I hope to see her.
Who has?	
Who has the hoe?	
Who has the house?	She hopes to hear from you.
Who has the harp?	We hope to receive them.
Who has the horse?	We hope to have them here.

(b) How did it happen?
How did you happen to hear it?
How did you happen to hear the remark?
Do you remember how it happened?
We happened to see them on the car.
I happened to hear about it.
That was before it happened.
Did you hear the story?
Did you hear the speech?
Did you hear both sides?
Did you hear both sides of the story?
Did you hear the report?
Did you hear the reply?
Did you hear the remark?
How did he behave?
I hope the boy will behave.

Help me.
You must help him.
You must help her.
Who will help them?
I hope that we can help him.
You must not refuse to help her.
Remember that you are to help them.
Have you heard about it?
Have you heard how happy they are?
Have you heard from home?
I have heard about it.
I have heard all about it.
I remember that I heard about it.

(c) Give the horse some hay.
We shall be happy to have you come.
I hope to hear from him before he goes South.
I hope he has not hurt himself.
He hopes to buy the house on the hill.
How many horses does he keep?
I happened to be in the house when she came to see my wife.
My wife happened to see the boy on the car.
If it is too heavy, I will help you.
I wish you would help me move the palm.
Heaven helps those who help themselves.
Have you heard how it happened that she came home from the South?
I happened to see her on the car.
If nothing happens, we shall go to the farm with them
She was very happy before it happened.
I hear that he will buy the house for his wife.

(d) The boy will show you the horse.
The house is on a high hill.
We have a fine view from the hill.
The house is half-way up the hill.
I hope they will not harm the horse.
He will show me how to play the hymn on the harp.

Come home with me.
If you will go with me I will show you the house.
Give me a piece of ham.
I have heard that they have a happy home.
The boy can help them hoe on the farm.
They may remain with you for an hour.
The car leaves on the half hour.
I believe it leaves here on the hour.
She was here an hour ago.
He hurt himself with the hoe.
I have heard that he will buy the house on the hill.
I saw the ship come into the harbor this morning.
There are five ships in the harbor.
I heard about it before they came home.

II. Vocabulary.

Use these words to form new sentences:

NOUNS AND PRONOUNS — harp, harm, home, hope, hoe, hoof, whole, hole, heap, house, hill, hall, horse, hymn, ham, whose, who, him, he.

VERBS — hurt, help, happen, hark, behave, rehearse.

ADJECTIVES OR ADVERBS — high, half-way, happy, however, how.

C — Exercise Story

There was once a crow.
Once upon a time there was a crow.
A long time ago there was a crow.
Where was the crow?
Did you see the crow?
Show me the crow.
Show me the crow on the tree.
The crow was on the tree.
The crow was sitting on the tree.
The crow was sitting on the high branch of a tree.

There was once a crow sitting on a high branch of the tree.

What kind of a tree was it?

Can you tell me what kind of a tree it was?

Did you notice what kind of a tree it was?

Did you notice that the crow was sitting on a high branch of the tree?

I saw the crow.

I noticed the crow.

I noticed that the crow held something in her bill.

What was it?

Did you notice what it was?

What was it that the crow held in her bill?

Did you notice what it was that the crow held in her bill?

It was a piece of cheese.

Are you fond of cheese?

The crow was very fond of cheese.

The crow was eating the cheese.

The crow had flown into the tree to eat the cheese.

Who saw the crow?

Who came along the road?

The fox came along the road.

The fox saw the crow.

The fox, too, was fond of cheese.

The fox liked cheese.

The fox was very hungry.

The fox was so hungry he longed for the cheese.

The fox is very sly.

He thought to himself, ...

He said to himself, ...

He said to himself, "I must have that cheese."

"How I should like to have that cheese!" said the fox to himself.

"How can I get it?"

"How can I get it away from the crow?"

"I know what I will do."

"I think I know how to get it."

The fox looked up at the crow.

The fox looked up at the crow and said, ...

"How do you do?"

"How are you?"

"I am glad to see you."

"I have wished to see you."

"I have wished for some time to see you."

"I have heard about you."

"Everyone is talking about you."

"All the birds of the forest are talking about you."

"All are talking about your beautiful voice."

"I have heard so much about your beautiful voice that I have come to hear you sing."

"Will you sing for me?"

"Will you please sing one song for me?"

"Will you have the kindness to sing for me?"

The crow was very much flattered.

The crow was so flattered....

The crow was so pleased....

The crow was so pleased with this flattery....

The crow was so pleased with this flattery that she opened her bill.

But the moment she opened her bill, the cheese dropped to the ground.

As soon as she opened her bill, she dropped the cheese.

She dropped the cheese the moment she opened her bill.

The fox picked up the cheese.

The fox did not wait for the crow to sing.

Without waiting for the crow to sing, the fox picked up the cheese and ran away.

THE FOX AND THE CROW

A crow had stolen a piece of cheese, and had flown up into the tree with it.

As she sat there on the bough, a fox came running along.

"O that cheese!" said he. "How good it smells! I will have it as I live."

So, coming close up under the tree, he said, "Dear Mrs. Crow, how beautiful you are! I did not know before that you were so beautiful. How bright your eyes are! And how your feathers shine in the sunlight!"

The silly old crow was flattered and began to rustle her feathers.

"I wonder if you can sing!" continued the fox. "I know you can! Of course you can! I do not doubt that you have the sweetest voice in all the forest. Please sing one note for me!"

"Caw! caw!" cried the crow.

"Ha, ha!" laughed the fox, as the cheese dropped from her bill. "Your voice is very good; and so is the cheese."

LESSON VI

A

I. **r** before a vowel.

The visible characteristic of **r** before a vowel is the forward movement of the lips.

rä, rō, rōō, rā, rē, röû, rī, röĭ, râ

II. **Mirror Practice:** —

1. Compare **r** with consonants of Class **I.**

fä‿rä	**sä‿rä**	**mä‿rä**
fō‿rō	**sō‿rō**	**mō‿rō**
fōō‿rōō	**sōō‿rōō**	**mōō‿rōō**
fā‿rā	**sā‿rā**	**mā‿rā**
fē‿rē	**sē‿rē**	**mē‿rē**
fī‿rī	**sī‿rī**	**mī‿rī**
föû‿röû	**söû‿röû**	**möû‿röû**
fâ‿râ	**sâ‿râ**	**mâ‿râ**

2. Difference between **r** and **k** (hard **c**, hard **ġ**).

Repeat rapidly in one breath: —
the **cā** the **cā** the **cā** — the **rā**

Notice that in both **cā** and **rā**, the mouth remains open. In **cā** we see the jaw movement; in **rā** the lips move forward.

Practice: —

the **case** the **case** the **case** — the **race**

Where is the **case?**
Where is the **race?**

3. Further comparison in the following sentences: —

I saw the **c**ase.
I saw the **r**ace.

We may **g**o.
We may **r**ow.
We may **m**ow.
We may **s**ew.
We may **sh**ow.

She may see the **m**ice.
She may see the **r**ice.

Do you see the **r**ail?
Do you see the **s**ail?

4. Syllable drill leading up to a sentence.

hē	**rō**			
hē	**ri**			
hē	**râ**			
hē	**roi**			
hē	**rōō**			
hē	**mā**	**rōō**		
hē	**mā**	**rē**		
sē	**mē**	**rē**		
sē	**mē**	**ri**		
shē	**sâ**	**mē**	**ri**	
wē	**mā**	**hē**	**ri**	
mā	**wē**	**sē**	**thē**	**ri**
mā	**wē**	**sē**	**thē**	**rō**

May we see the rose?

B

I. Sentence Practice.

(a) Can you read?
Will you read?

May I read?
Shall I read?
Do you read?
Did you read?
Did you read this?
Did you read it?
Did you read it to him? to her?
Did they read it to you?
Did she read it over?
Can you read it to me?
May I read this to you?
Will you read to him?
I will read to him.
I can read it to him.
They may write.
They will write.
They can write.
They shall write.
What shall they write?
What can I write?
What will you write?
What may they write?
What did they write?
What have they written?
What has she written?
Have you read what she has written?
Have you heard what she has written?
Have you read over what she has written?
Have you read through what she has written?
Have you re-read what she has written?
Will you read me what she has written?
Will you let me read what she has written?
Will you let me read over what she has written?
Will you let me read through what she has written?
Who wrote what she read?
Who read what she wrote?

(b) Is it right?
Is it wrong?

It is not wrong.
It was not right.
What she wrote was not right.
What she wrote was not read over.
What she wrote was not well written.
Will you reply to what she wrote?
Who will write to them?
Who will read to them?
Who can read to me?
Who will write this letter
Write it for me.
You must write to me.
That is right.
That is the right way.
She said that was the right way.
He said he would show me the right way.
He said he would show the boy how to read and write.
Do you believe that he will be able to read that?
I hope that I shall have time to read it over before I go.
I have not written to him for some time.
It was of no use to write to them.
If I were in your place, I should write to them about it at once.

(c) Did you read the letter?
Did you read the paper?
Did you read the "Review"?
Did you read the book?
You must remember what you read.
I wish you would read to me.
You must not read so much.
You will hurt your eyes if you read so much.
What paper did you read?
Please give me something to read.
Shall we ride or walk?
I would rather ride.
Is this the right way to the river?
You are right and I am wrong.

Write the report before you go.
I will write to you when I arrive.
Will you go for a row with me?
Have you heard the rhyme?
I will read the rhyme to you.
You are wrong. That is not the right way to the river.
What did they raise on the farm?
Do you think it will rain?
I hope it will not rain before we get home.
They came home in the rain.
If it rains, we cannot go for a row on the river.

(d) The river is rough.
If the river is rough, we shall not go for a row.
Shall we row to the ship?
How much did you pay for those red roses?
My wife gave the boy a red rose.
We found the roses beside the road.
When did the boy arrive at the farm?
We saw him when he arrived in Rome.
I shall hear from him when he arrives in Cairo.
We have no room for him.
What kind of paper do you wish for your room?
They have raised the rent of the house.
We heard that the boy ran away from the farm.
I wish you would show me how to write the report.
When you have time you must read his book on Rome.
They wrote us that they had seen the river Rhine.
I wish you would read the rest of it.
You must rest your eyes before you read the paper.
Where did you buy the rug for your room?
What size is the rug in your room?
That is not the right size.

II. Vocabulary.

These words may be used to form new sentences:

Nouns — rose, race, rail, rainbow, rake, raven, ray, ream, reason, reef, rhyme, rice, Rome, Cairo, rock, road, river, rope, row, rye, Roy.

Verbs — raise, reach, read, reap, rise, ride, write, roam, run.

Adjectives or Adverbs — rare, rear, rich, wrong, ripe.

C — Exercise Story

An old man had a bird.

An old man had a parrot.

Once an old man had a parrot to sell.

Once an old man had a parrot for sale.

Once an old man had a parrot that he wished to sell.

The parrot could speak.

The man had taught the parrot to speak.

The man had taught the parrot to say one sentence.

The man had taught the parrot to say this one sentence, "There is no doubt about it."

An old man who had a parrot to sell had taught him to say this one sentence, "There is no doubt about it."

Then he took the parrot out into the street.

Then he took the parrot out into the street where many people passed by.

The old man asked everyone who passed by....

The old man asked all who came by if they wished to buy the bird.

"Do you wish to buy a fine parrot?" said the old man to all who passed by.

"Will you please buy my parrot?" said the old man.

But no one wanted the bird.

Finally, one day,....

At length, one day....

At length, one day a man came by.

At length, one day a man came by who took a fancy to the bird.

The stranger looked at the bird.

The stranger looked at the bird and then said to the old man,....

"How much do you want for your parrot?"

The old man replied, "I want ten dollars."

The old man replied, "I will sell him for ten dollars."

The stranger looked at the bird and said, "Are you worth it?"

The parrot replied, ""There is no doubt about it."

The man was so pleased with the reply....

The man was so pleased with the answer....

The man was so pleased with the answer that he bought the bird.

He took him home and thought he could talk more.

He took him home and tried to make him talk more.

But the parrot could only say this one sentence.

The man was disappointed — angry — very angry.

He said, "What a fool I was to pay ten dollars for you."

He said, "What a fool I was to pay so much for you."

The bird replied, "There is no doubt about it."

THE PARROT

Once an old man had a parrot that he wished to sell. He had taught the parrot to say the sentence, "There is no doubt about it."

Then he took the parrot out into the street where many people passed by. He asked everyone, "Do you wish to buy a fine parrot?" But no one wanted the bird.

Finally, one day, a man came along who took a fancy to the bird. He asked the price of the parrot. The old man said, "I will sell him to you for ten dollars."

The stranger looked at the bird and said, "Are you worth it?"

The parrot replied, "There is no doubt about it."

The man was so pleased with this reply that he bought the bird. He took him home expecting that he could talk more. But the parrot could only say this one sentence.

The man was so disappointed and he said to himself, "What a fool I was to pay ten dollars for you."

The bird replied, "There is no doubt about it."

And the bird was right.

LESSON VII

A

I. **r** after a vowel.

The movement for **r** after a vowel varies. Often we see no other movement besides the vowel. Sometimes we see a downward movement and sometimes we see the tip of the tongue slightly raised forming a glide **r.**

II. Mirror Practice on Sounds.

Note. So much depends upon the word that follows the final letter **r,** that we practice no syllables in this lesson.

B

I. Sentence Practice.

(a) Where is....
Where was....
Where were....

There were....
There was....
There is....
Here is....
Here was....
Here were....

Who was here?
Who was there?
Were you there?
Were they here?
When were they here?
When were you there?

I was there before you.
She was here before you came.
He will be there.
Be sure to go there.
He will be sure to go.
He will be sure to say so to them.
He will be sure to write to them.
They will be sure to read the letter.
Be sure to buy some more.

Shall I buy much more?
Shall I write much more?
Shall I read much more?
Do you believe that she will give me much more?
Do you believe there is much more?
There were a few more.

I believe there were a few more.
I believe there were four more.
I am sure there were four more.
I am sure there were four or more.
I must write four letters.
I must write four more.

You are right. There were more.
Are you sure that there were more?
I cannot remember how many there were.
I believe there were four or five.
I believe there were four or five more.

(b) How far did you go?
Is it far off?
Is it far away?
Is it far from here?
How far is it from here?
How far is it to the car?
How far did you ride on the car?
How far does this car go?
What is the fare on the car?
Have you paid your fare?

Will you pay my fare?
Will you give me my share?
Are you sure that this is the right car?

Be sure to go to the fair.
Be sure to come early.
Be sure to go with them.
Be sure to reply.
Be sure to remember what he says.
Be sure to tell me all about it.
Be sure to be there on time.
Be sure to see them all.
Be sure to find out about it.

Do you care to hear about it?
Do you care for more?
Do you care to see it?
Do you care to go to the fair?
Do you care to go there?

(c) There is some sugar for your coffee.
There is no more.
There is something wrong about it.
There is the book that I wish to read.
There is my father.
There is a rose on my rosebush.

Here is a rose for your mother.
Here is the house that I wish to buy.
Here is some paper for you.
Here are my rubbers.

Where are they?
Where were they?
Where were the papers?
Where were you when they came?

Come here.
Who is here? Who was there?
What did you hear about it?
How did she hear about it?

You will hear from me before long.
How did she appear?
They appear to be very happy in their new home.
I would rather go with her.
We were there for over an hour.
I am sure that it was more than an hour.

(d) Do you care to go there?
Did you pay my car-fare?
What did she wear when she went to the fair with you?
I must buy a pair of shoes and a pair of rubbers to wear at the sea-shore.
What did you buy at the fair?
Did you hire a house at the sea-shore for the summer?
I read in the paper that the house is for sale.
I shall not go before supper.
We must go to the pier to see the ship before supper.
Do you remember the way to the pier?
I hope they will offer to show me the way to the fair.
You may refer to me if you wish.
I shall offer to go to the farm for her, if the weather is fair.
What year was it that they went to the sea-shore with us?
It was the same year they came from Rome.
I don't remember what year it was.
They came in by the rear door, so that I did not hear them.

II. Vocabulary.

These words may be used to form new sentences.

NOUNS — car, oar, core, fare (fair), bear, hair (hare), care, air, pear, mare, fear, beer, pier, hour, power, shower, fire.

VERBS — care, fare, pare, share, wear, fear, shear.

ADJECTIVES OR ADVERBS. — where, whereabout, sheer, far, more, four, here, there.

C — Exercise Story

I write.
They write.
They write to me.
They will write to me.
They may write to her.
Will you write?
Will you write to me?
Will you write to me before you go?
Write to me as soon as you can — arrive.
I have written the letter — exercise — report.
She wrote the exercise.
She wrote the letter to her friend.
Did you write your letter this morning?
As soon as she writes to me I will let you know.
Probably he will write to them before he goes.
What did he write?
Why did he write to his friend?

He wrote to his friend because he had forgotten his umbrella at his house.

When he found that he had left his umbrella at his friend's house he wrote to him.

He wrote to him at once.

Immediately he wrote a note to him.

He immediately wrote a note to his friend asking him to send the umbrella that he had left at his house.

Have you heard the story?

Have you heard the story about the man who thought that he had left his umbrella at his friend's house?

So he wrote a note.

So he wrote a note asking him to return the umbrella by the bearer of the note.

He wrote a note saying — "I have left my umbrella at your house. Will you please be kind enough to send me the same by the bearer of the note?"

He closed the letter.

He was about to seal the letter.

When he was about to seal the letter....

Just as he was about to seal the letter he found the umbrella.

So he added a postscript.

He took the letter and added the following postscript.

He added this postscript. "I have found my umbrella so do not take the trouble to look for it."

As I have found my umbrella you need not take the trouble to look for it.

Then he closed the letter.

After closing the letter — note....

Then after closing the letter, he sealed it and sent it to his friend.

Just before closing the letter, he found the umbrella so he added a postscript, saying, "I have just found my umbrella, so I will not trouble you to look for it."

THE POSTSCRIPT

One day a gentleman went to call on his friend. When he returned home he thought that he had left his umbrella at the friend's house.

So he wrote him a note saying, "I have left my umbrella at your house, will you please be kind enough to send the same to me, by the bearer of the note?"

Before he had a chance to send the letter, he found his umbrella. He took the note, opened it, and added the following postscript:

"As I have just found my umbrella, do not take the trouble to look for it." Then he closed the letter and sent it to his friend.

LESSON VIII

A

I. **r** after **f, b, p** and **th.**

fr, br (**pr**), **thr** show a forward movement of the lips. If the vowel demands a forward movement as in the case of **frō** and **frōō** or **brō** and **brōō,** the vowel sound is simply retarded.

II. Mirror Practice on Sounds.

1. Difference between **f** and **fr,** etc.

Pronounce rapidly in one breath: —

fāfāfā — **frā**
fōfōfō — **frō**
fēfēfē — **frē**

Notice the forward movement in syllables containing the **r** before the vowel.

Notice the same in: —

the **fā**‿the **fā** ‿the **fā** ——— the **frame**
the **böû**‿the **böû**‿the **böû** ——— the **brow**
the **fēē**‿the **fēē** ‿the **fēē** ——— the **free**
the **bī**‿the **bī** ‿the **bī** ——— the **bribe**

2. Difference between

fä‿**frä**	föû‿**fröû**
fō‿**frō**	fâ‿**frâ**
fōō‿**frōō**	———
fā‿**frā**	bä‿**brä**
fē‿**frē**	bō‿**brō**
fī‿**frī**	etc.

3. Further comparison.

Repeat rapidly in one breath: — Notice forward movement in syllables containing **r.**

sō‿fē	sō‿bī	so‿bā
sō‿frē	sō‿brī	sō‿brā
mā‿fī	sā‿böû	mā‿fā
mā‿frī	sā‿bröû	mā‿frā
sō‿bē‿brē	sā‿bē‿fē	sā‿bē‿bā
sō‿bē‿brī	sā‿bē‿frē	sā‿bē‿brā
sō‿bē‿frē	sā‿bē‿bō	sō‿bē‿bā
sō‿bē‿frī	sā‿bē‿brō	sō‿bē‿brā

4. Syllable drill leading up to a sentence.

wē	**mā**	
mā	**thā**	
thā	**fō**	
thā	**frō**	
thā	**fou**	
shē	**fou**	
shē	**mā**	**frou**
shē	**mā**	**rō**
mā	**shē**	**bri**
wē	**mā**	**boi**
thā	**mā**	**broi**

They may broil the fish.

B

I. Sentence Practice.

(a) Throw it away.
Throw it back.
Throw it off.

Throw it to me.
Throw it over.
Throw it down.
Throw it up into the air.
Why do you throw it away?
I will throw it away.
She threw it down to me.
He threw it away.
I would throw that away if I were you.
Throw it away at once.
How far can you throw the ball?
When will you be through?
They will surely be through by that time.
I shall be through in half an hour.
We shall probably be through by three.
She was here from three to four.
How far is it from here to there?
How far is it from there to the pier?
The boy was here from four to five.
Come from three to four.
They came from far and near.
We saw the ship from afar.
The ship was far from the shore.

(b) Where is my frame?
What kind of a frame have you?
What is the price of the frame?
I saw the frame.
I will carve a frame for you.
He showed me the brown frame.
I will have it framed.
I am afraid.
I am afraid I have no more.
What are you afraid of?
I broke my frame.
I am afraid that he will break it.
Do not break it.
Break it off.
Break it off in two.

Break it in halves.
She broke the cake in halves.
Can you break it in halves for me?
Be careful not to break it.
Who broke my brown frame?
The boy was very brave.
Be brave.
Be brief.
You must write a brief report.
The report must be brief.

(c) Bring me the frame.
Bring me the book.
Bring me the report.
Bring me the broom.
Bring me the fruit.
Bring me some fresh fruit.
Bring me a good broom.
Bring me a brief report.
Bring me a brown frame.
Bring it to me.
Bring it with you when you come.
Have you brought it with you?
Have you brought the report with you?
Be sure to bring it with you.
It must be brief.
I shall be free from three to five.
Did the boy get the prize?
Who offered the prize?
He is very proud.
We are proud of her.
I shall go more frequently from now on.
He goes to see them from time to time.
The boy brought some fresh fruit from the farm.
He brought home the paper.

(d) Show me the brown frame that you bought.
Did you have the picture framed?
Did you make this frame or did you buy it?
I am afraid I cannot go, as I promised to be at home from three to four.

Will you buy a loaf of bread for me when you go out?
Will you have a piece of brown bread and some fruit?
Are you fond of fruit-cake?
She wore a brown hat with a broad brim.
The broad brim will shade your eyes.
What is the price of the brown hat in the window?
That is too high-priced for my means.
The boy is very proud of the prize that he won at school.
Will you write a brief report before to-morrow?
Remember that the report is to be very brief and that it is to be ready before Friday.
Come promptly on Friday and bring the frame with you.
Bring me the book after you have read it.
I saw a bird on the branch of the fruit-tree.
The boys have been fishing in the brook.
How far is it from here to the brook?
How long will it take to walk to the brook?
That was a surprise.
It was a surprise to see them on Friday.
Can you prove that?
Show me the proof.
How can you prove that you are right?

II. Vocabulary.

These words may be used to form new sentences:

NOUNS — frame, freight, friend, fright, fruit, bread, breath, breeze, bridge, brush, prey, praise, prose.

VERBS — fry, break, broke, prey, bring, preach, pray.

ADJECTIVES — free, fresh, brave, brief, bright, proud, three.

C — Exercise Story

This story is about Benjamin Franklin.
Who was Benjamin Franklin?
Benjamin Franklin was a famous philosopher and statesman.

Where did he live?

He lived in Philadelphia.

Philadelphia is an interesting city.

Many interesting stories are told about Benjamin Franklin.

One evening......

One evening some people were in a room of a hotel.

How many people were in the room?

Twenty persons were sitting in a room talking together.

One man had a fine watch.

It was a gold watch.

The watch was gold.

Somebody stole the watch out of the man's pocket.

The man missed the watch.

He told the people in the room that somebody had stolen his watch out of his pocket.

They did not know who the thief was.

Just then Benjamin Franklin came in.

They told him what had happened.

He said that he could find the thief.

He told the men to shut the doors.

Then he called the landlord.

He called the landlord and told him to bring him something.

What was it?

It was a brass kettle.

The landlord brought the brass kettle.

Then Franklin told him to bring a rooster.

The landlord brought the rooster.

The men looked on in surprise.

They did not know what Franklin would do.

They did not know what Franklin would do with the kettle and the rooster.

They could not imagine what he would do.

They could not imagine what he intended to do.

Franklin took the kettle.

He turned the kettle upside down and put the rooster under it.

Then he blew out the lights.

He told the men to walk around the kettle.

He told them to walk around the kettle and touch the bottom of it with their hands.

Franklin said that when the thief touched the kettle the rooster would crow.

The men laughed.

The men laughed, but they all walked around the kettle and each man put his hand on it.

Then Franklin lighted the lamps.

He told the men to hold up their hands.

He looked at them.

They all had black hands except one man.

His hands were clean.

The men searched him and found the stolen watch.

The thief thought that the rooster would really crow if he touched the kettle.

So he only pretended to touch it.

The other men all had black hands.

The innocent men all had black hands because the bottom of the kettle was black and sooty.

CATCHING A THIEF

The following story is told about Benjamin Franklin. One evening a number of men were talking together in a room of a hotel. Suddenly one of them missed his watch. The man was sure it had been stolen out of his pocket. He told the other men what had happened.

Just then Benjamin Franklin entered the room. He said that he could find the thief. He told the men to close the doors. Then he called the landlord and told him to bring him a large brass kettle and a rooster. When the landlord brought the kettle and the rooster, Franklin turned the kettle upside down and put the rooster under it. Then he blew out the lights and told all the men to walk around the kettle and touch it with their hands. He said, "When the thief touches the kettle the rooster will crow."

The men were very much amused, but they all did as they were told.

Then Franklin lighted the lamps and told the men to hold up their hands. They all had black hands except one man. The men searched him and found the stolen watch. The thief thought that the rooster would really crow if he touched the kettle so he only pretended to do so. The innocent men all had black hands, because the bottom of the kettle was black and sooty.

LESSON IX

A

I. **r** after **c** and **ġ.**

cr and **ġr** have the same forward movement as the combinations of the preceding lesson.

Note. As **cr** and **ġr** look alike, we practice only one of these in syllables.

II. Mirror Practice on Sounds.

1. Difference between: —

cä‿**cr**ä	ke(cē)‿**cr**ē
cō‿**cr**ō	kī‿**cr**ī
cōō‿**cr**ōō	cöû‿**cr**öû
cā‿**cr**ā	câ‿**cr**â

Notice the forward movement in syllables containing **r** before the vowel.

2. Further Comparisons.

Pronounce rapidly: —

the **cr**ā — the cā
crō — the cǫ
cröû — the cöw
crōō — the cōō
crī — the kī
crâ — the câ

3. Practice: —

See the cape.	Keep away.
See the crape (or grape).	Creep away.
Show me the cane.	Where is the cave.
Show me the crane.	Where is the grave?

Note. Remember to speak perfectly naturally and as rapidly as possible in practising all exercises before the mirror, and also insist upon this when others are giving the sentences.

4. Syllable drill leading up to a sentence.

mi	**kē**	
mi	**crou**	
mi	**crē**	
thā	**crē**	
thā	**cri**	
whi	**thā**	**cri**
wē	**mā**	**fri**
wē	**fli**	
wē	**sâ**	
hōō	**sâ**	

Who saw the crow fly away?

B

I. Sentence Practice.

(a) It grows.
It grew.
How it grows!
How it has grown!
How it grew!
The flowers grew.
The flowers grew by the roadside.

The flowers grew in the garden.
Where does it grow?
Can you tell me where it grows?
Can you tell me where this flower grows?
It grew by the river.
It grew by the roadside.
It grows in the South.
I believe it grows in the South.
I have seen it a great many times.
I have a great many more.
There were a great many more.
I am sure there were a great many more
We have been there a great many times.
She writes a great deal.
She reads a great deal.
She spends a great deal of time reading.
That would be a great deal worse.
It would be a great deal better to do it now.

(b) Cross it out.
Cross over to the other side.
Cross the river.
Cross the street.
Cross the ocean.
She was so cross this morning.
He was cross because I criticised him.
That is wrong; cross it out.
Shall we cross over to the other side?
Shall we row across the river?
I crossed the ocean a great many years ago.
How did you happen to come across the book?
They live in the house across the way.
Did you hear the cry?
They cried for help.
The children were playing by the creek.
One of the children fell into the creek.
Did you hear the child cry when it fell into the creek?
Can you crochet?
Can you play croquet?
Will you have a game of croquet?

The children were playing croquet on the grass.

(c) Will you have some grapes?
Are you fond of grape-fruit?
Are the grapes ripe?
Have you a grape-vine in your garden?
Shall we go to the grove?
There is a fine grove behind our house.
The farmer has raised a fine crop of grain.
What kind of grain do they use to make flour?
The grain is ripe.
The grapes are ripe.
When the grapes are ripe I will bring you some.
I prefer the grape-fruit.
Will you have some cream?
I prefer the cream in my coffee.
The cream is sour.
We have fresh cream from the farm every morning.
The boy brings the cream and the fruit from the farm.
I saw a crow on the branch of the tree.
Do you remember the story about the crow?
The crow is a bird.
The crane is a bird.
I saw the crane in the water.

(d) There were a great many grapes on the vine.
We have a great deal of work to do.
It would be a great mistake to do that.
The ship has gone on a cruise around the world.
How large is the ship's crew?
Was the crew saved when the ship sank?
She was very cross when I criticised her work.
He will be cross if you criticise him.
They live in the brown house across the way.
The car was crowded this morning.
Did you see the crowd on the street this morning?
How the boy grows?
I wish you would bring me some grapes from your vine.

We have a great many grapes on our grape-vine this year.
I bought some grape-fruit at the fruit-store.
What kind of grapes do they use to make wine?
We must make a fire in the grate.
The ground is frozen.
You must take the green car.
The green car passes our house.
How far is it from here to the green house?
I saw them grow in the green house across the way.

II. Vocabulary.

These words may be used to form new sentences:

NOUNS — crane, cream, creek, crew, crib, croquet, croup, crow, grain, grammar, grape, grass, grandmother, grandfather, Greek, Greece, grief, grocer, groom, groove, growth.

VERBS — croak, crave, crawl, creep, crochet, grow, grew, grope.

ADJECTIVES — cross, grave, green, gray, great.

C — Exercise Story

Did you ring the bell?
Did you hear the bell ring?
Who rang the bell?
Did the visitor ring the bell?
Does the bell ring often?
I do not like to have the bell ring often.
It annoys me to have the bell ring often.
Who answered the bell?
Who went to the door?
Who came to the door when you rang the bell?
A visitor was at the door.
A gentleman was often annoyed by a visitor.
Do you know the person at the door?
Who is the person at the door?
I am expecting a visitor.

I am annoyed by that visitor.

I am annoyed by the visit of a tiresome person.

A gentleman was often annoyed by the visit of a tiresome person.

The gentleman did not wish to see this man.

He told his servant not to admit him again.

Finally he ordered his servant not to admit this man again.

One day......

One day the bell rang.

One day the bell rang and the servant went to the door.

Then the servant went to the door......

When the servant opened the door......

When the servant opened the door he saw the unwelcome visitor.

The latter asked the servant......

The latter asked the servant, "Is your master at home?"

The servant wanted to be polite.

The servant wished to be polite.

The servant wished to dismiss him politely.

When the unwelcome visitor asked the servant, "Is your master at home?" the latter, wishing to dismiss him politely, said that he was out.

Then the visitor said, "Is your mistress at home?"

The visitor said to the servant, "Tell your mistress that I would like to see her."

"I would like to see your mistress. I have something important to tell her."

The servant replied, "She is out, too."

Did the visitor go away then?

Did he leave then?

No, he did not go away.

He wished to wait for them.

He said he would wait for them.

It is very cold today.

It is so cold I cannot wait outside.

It is too cold to wait on the street.

As it is so cold I will come in.

I will come in and sit down by the fire.

As it is so cold, I will come in and take a seat by the fire.

The visitor said to the servant, "It is too cold to wait outside, may I come in and sit down by the fire?"

But the servant said, "I'm sorry, that's out, too."

"Oh," replied the servant with the greatest calmness, "That's out, too."

THAT IS OUT, TOO

A gentleman was often annoyed by a tedious visitor. He told his servant never to let this person into the house again. When the unwelcome visitor came and asked the servant, "Is your master at home?" the servant replied politely that he was out. Then the visitor remarked: "Tell your mistress that I would like to see her, as I have something to say to her." The servant answered that she, too, was out. The visitor then said that he would wait for her, but as it was cold, he would take a seat by the fire in the parlor. But the servant replied, with the greatest calmness: "That is out, too."

LESSON X

A

I. **l** after **f, s, b** (**p**) at the beginning of a word.

fl, sl, bl, (pl). In pronouncing **l,** the tip of the tongue is placed against the upper gum. Generally the action of the tongue is seen. The vowel movement is somewhat prolonged in syllables containing the **l** after **f, s, b** (**p**).

II. Mirror Practice.

1. Difference between: —

fä‿**fl**ä	sä‿**sl**ä	bä‿**bl**ä
fō‿**fl**ō	sō‿**sl**ō	bō‿**bl**ō
fōō‿**fl**ōō	sōō‿**sl**ōō	bōō‿**bl**ōō
fā‿**fl**ā	sā‿**sl**ā	bā‿**bl**ā
fē‿**fl**ē	sē‿**sl**ē	bē‿**bl**ē
föû‿**fl**öû	söû‿**sl**öû	böû‿**bl**öû
fī‿**fl**ī	sī‿**sl**ī	bī‿**bl**ī
fīr‿**fl**īr	sīr‿**sl**ür	bür‿**bl**ür

2. Pronounce rapidly: —

Notice tongue movement in syllables containing **l.**

She may pay.	That may be so.
She may **pl**ay.	That may be **sl**ow.

the bow — the **bl**ow
the burr — the **bl**ur
the feet — the **fl**eet
the soap — the **sl**ope
the soup — the **sl**oop

3. Difference between **fr** and **fl,** and between **br** and **bl.**

Pronounce rapidly: —

the **frame** — the **flame**
the **fruit** — the **flute**
the **fright** — the **flight**
the **broom** — the **bloom**

Notice that in **frame** we see a forward movement before the vowel, and in **flame** we see the movement of the tongue before the vowel, etc.

4. Syllable drill leading up to a sentence.

sē	**thē**	**blōō**
sē	**thē**	**bē**
sē	**thē**	**si**
sē	**thē**	**ki**
sē	**thē**	**fli**
sē	**thē**	**sur**
sē	**thē**	**fē**
sē	**thē**	**sli**
sē	**thē**	**brā**
sē	**thē**	**crō**
sē	**thē**	**flou**

Did you see the flower there?

B

I. Sentence Practice.

(a) **Will you play?**
Can you play?
Did you play?
Did she play?
Did she play for you?
How did he play?
Shall I play to you?
Let me play.

Let us play.
Let us go to the play.
Let us go to see the play.
Let us go to see the play tomorrow afternoon.
What play did you see?
What play did they give?
Did you say that the play was good?
Shall we ask them to go to the play with us?
What place is this?
Is this the place you mean?
Please show me the place.
The place is far away.
The place I mean is far away.
I am sure that you will find it in the same place.
I shall be pleased to see them.
They were pleased to receive the flowers.
Please play that over and play it more slowly.

(b) How did you sleep?
Did you sleep well?
I was very sleepy this afternoon.
She is very slow about it.
Slow but sure.
Please show me the place.
There is a sloop in the harbor.
Did you see the sloop?
Who was to blame?
He always blames me.
How could you blame him!
Have you found out who was to blame?
The bird flew away.
The bluebird flew to and fro.
The wind blows.
How the wind blew!
This blue flower grew by the roadside.
The name of the play was "The Bluebird."
Have you ever read the story of "Bluebeard?"
The water is so blue.
Blue is very becoming to her.
She wore a black hat with a plume.

I bought a beautiful blue plume.
Blow the flame.
"Little Boy Blue come blow your horn."

(c) The farmer has a flock of sheep.
I saw a flock of birds fly away.
A flock of birds flew South.
The phlox is a beautiful flower.
The flax has a blue flower.
Where does the flax grow?
Have you ever seen a field of flax in bloom?
My rose-bush is in bloom.
The farmer ploughs the field.
Will you help me plant the rose-bush?
Where shall we plant it?
My plants thrive well.
Will you go for a sleigh-ride with me?
Are you fond of sleighing?
Give me a slice of bread.
The fox is very sly.
If you are so slow you will not be through in time.
He plays too slowly.
How slowly the river flows!
The slaves were set free.

(d) I will play to you for an hour this afternoon.
Are you going to take part in the play?
They always play very well.
She wore her new blue hat to the play.
Her new black hat is too large.
A blue hat with a plume would be becoming to her.
I prefer the blue one.
I shall buy the black one.
Have you heard him play the flute?
They say he plays the flute well.
We heard the blind man play the flute on the street.
Can you replace them?
Place the vase on the floor.
Was it a blackbird or a bluebird?
The wind blew the ships far out to sea.

Which way does the wind blow?
I saw a fleet of warships in the harbor.
The fleet was far from the shore.
There is a high bluff by the river.
Will you walk to the bluff with me?
Shall we walk to the bluff, or do you prefer to ride?
Ask him to give you the black frame for the picture.
Which do you prefer, the black frame or the brown one?
Will you give me the pleasure of your company to tea this afternoon?
It will give me much pleasure to go to the play with you.

II. Vocabulary.

These words may be used to form new sentences:

NOUNS — flame, flaw, fleece, fleet, flea, flight, flirt, floor, flour, flower, fly, blame, blaze, place, blouse, blow, blur, plough, plume.

VERBS — bloom, blow, plough, play, blame, blur, ply.

ADJECTIVES — blithe, blue, plain.

C — Exercise Story

The fox fell into the well.
The fox fell into the water.
The fox fell into an old well.
The fox fell into a deep well.
The sly fox fell into a deep well.
One day a sly old fox fell into the water.
He could not climb out of the well.
He was unable to climb out of the well.
Who saw the fox?
Who saw the fox fall into the well?
Who happened to see the fox fall into the water?
Who chanced to see the fox fall into the water?

Who chanced to pass by?

Who happened to pass by at that moment?

A goat happened to pass by.

A goat who chanced to pass by the well saw the fox.

A goat who chanced to be passing by at that moment saw the fox in the well.

The goat looked at the fox.

The goat looked down at the fox.

The goat spoke to the fox.

The goat asked the fox......

"What are you doing?"

"What are you doing down there in the water?"

The fox replied,......

The fox looked up at the goat.

The fox cried to the goat,......

"Come and have some water."

"Come and have a drink of water."

"Come and have a drink of this clear water."

"Come and have a drink of this clear cool water."

"Come and have a taste of this clear cool water."

"Come and taste this clear cool water."

"You have never tasted such good water."

"You have never tasted such clear cool water."

"I am sure you have never tasted such fine water."

"Surely you have never tasted such fine water."

"You must have a taste."

"Will you have a drink?"

"Will you have a taste?"

"Come and have a sip of it."

The fox looked up at the goat and said, "This is surely the best water I have ever tasted. Come and have a drink of it."

"Come down and I will give you a drink."

"Do come down and I will give you a drink."

So the goat jumped down.

So the goat jumped down into the water.

So the silly goat jumped down into the water.

He found the water good.

He found the water to be as good as the fox had said.

He said, "This is good water."

"This is indeed good water."
"Indeed this is fine water."
"I was very thirsty."
"I was very thirsty and this water is delicious."
The fox said, "You may drink all you want."
"Drink as much as you wish."
"Drink as much as you want."
"Please drink all you want."
When the fox said this,......
As the fox said this,......
While saying this,......
While saying this, the fox jumped upon the goat's back.
As he said this, the fox jumped upon the goat's back.
He leaped on the goat's back.
He leaped on the goat's back and then on his horns.
From there he leaped to the top of the well.
From there he reached the top of the well.
From there he could reach the top of the well.
From there he could leap to the top of the well.
From there he could leap to the curb of the well.
Then he looked back into the well.
Then he looked back into the well at the goat.
Then he called back to the goat.
"Good-bye, Mr. Goat."
"Good-bye, Mr. Goat, I hope you will get all the water you wish."
"I hope you will be able to quench your thirst, and then be able to find your way out."
"I hope after quenching your thirst, you will be able to find your way out of the well."
He left the goat.
He did not wait for the goat.
He left the goat to find his way out as best he could.
He went away and left the goat to his fate.

THE FOX IN THE WELL

A sly old fox fell into a well, and could not climb out.

"What are you doing down there?" asked a goat who chanced to be passing by.

"Oh, such clear cold water!" cried the fox. "The nicest water I ever tasted! Come and have a sip of it."

So down jumped the silly goat. "This is good water," said he, "and I was very thirsty."

"Pray drink all you want," said the fox. And as he said this, he leaped upon the goat's back, then to his horns, then upon the curb of the well, and out upon the ground.

"Good-day, Mr. Goat," said he, "I hope you will get all the water you want."

And away he went, leaving the goat to find his way out as best he could.

LESSON XI

A

I. l after **c** and **ġ** at the beginning of a word.

cl and **ġl** have the same tongue movement as in the combinations of the preceding lesson. In **cl** and **ġl,** however, only the **l** is visible while in **fl, bl, pl** and **sl** movement for both consonants is seen.

Note. As **cl** and **ġl** look alike we practice only one of these in syllables.

II. Mirror Practice.

1. Difference between syllables without **l** and with **l:** —

cä‿clä	kī‿klī
cō‿clō	cöû‿clöû
cōō‿clōō	cöĭ‿clöĭ
cā‿clā	cür‿clẽr
kē‿klē	câ‿clâ

2. Pronounce rapidly and note the difference: —

the cove — the **cl**ove
the coke — the **cl**oak
the kirk — the **cl**erk
the game — the **cl**aim
the cause — the **cl**ause

3. Difference between **cr** and **cl:** —

the **cr**ew — the **cl**ue
the **ġr**ove — the **cl**ove
the **cr**ime — the **cl**imb
the **ġr**oom — the **ġl**oom

Notice in **cr**ew we see the forward movement before the vowel and in **cl**ue the movement of the tongue before the vowel, etc.

4. Syllable drill leading up to a sentence.

thē clä
thē cä
thē clōō
thē crōō
thē crâ
mi clâ
mi kē
mi cli
mi clō

My cloak is blue.

B

I. Sentence Practice.

(a) Close the window.
Close the door.
Close the shop.
Close up the house.
Close the office.
Have they closed the shop?
What time do they close the office?
The room is very close.
It is very close here.
Come in and close the door.
They close the shop at five o'clock.
I am glad you came.
I shall be glad to go.
They will be glad to come.
He will be glad to see you.
We shall be glad to hear from you.
I am glad that it is true.
You will be glad to hear that they are coming.
Shall we climb the hill?
Did you climb the cliff?
Can you climb up?
If you climb to the top of the hill, you will have a clear view.

It was too warm to climb the hill.
Do you think we shall have clear weather?
It is not very clear this morning.
The house is on a high cliff.

(b) There is a clock in the other room.
Is your clock right?
That clock may be slow.
Who gave you the clock in your room?
I must have my clock repaired.
That is very pretty cloth.
The cloak was made of blue broadcloth.
Will you buy some more black cloth?
What is the price of the black broadcloth cloak?
My sister gave me a pair of gloves.
She brought the gloves from Paris.
Where are your gloves?
What size gloves do you wear?
I wear a five and a half glove.
Does he wear glasses?
He has broken his glasses.
He cannot see to read without his glasses.
Be careful not to break your glasses.
I broke a glass globe this morning.
Will you buy a globe for me when you go out?
What kind of a globe do you want?
Where is my clothes-brush?
You will find it in the closet.
My cloak is in my closet.
Give me my cloak.

(c) What do they claim?
They claim that it is not right.
Who claimed the book?
He claims that he found it there.
Please give me a glass of water.
Be careful not to break the glass.
It was made of glass.
Have you ever seen the glass flowers?
She came to our class.

What time does the class meet?
Where does the class meet?
He was a class-mate of mine.
They were class-mates.
They have found a clue.
Will you go to the club with me?
Where is the Club-house?
The Club-house is on the cliff.
The boy belongs to the club.
I shall be glad to go to the club with you.
Please show me the way to the Club-house.
I found the gloves at the club.
He lost his glasses on the way to the club.
Who claimed the glasses that were found at the Club-house?

(d) Shall we climb the hill today or tomorrow?
Perhaps we can walk to the cliff with them, if they care to walk so far.
If we go to the sea-shore we must have some clams.
Did you ever go to a clam-bake?
He promised to be here by five o'clock so that we could go to the club together.
Come in and close the door.
He came to town in the closed car this morning.
Can you tell me at what time the bank closes?
We shall be glad to go if it is not too cold.
We were so glad to hear from him.
I am sure they will be glad to help you.
I am glad nothing happened to him.
Where can I have my gloves cleaned?
Has anyone claimed the watch that was found at the club?
That was a clever reply.
He made a clever remark.
Did you ever find a four-leafed clover?
Are you fond of cloves?
Did you speak to the clerk about the gloves?
You will find some glue in the closet.

II. Vocabulary.

These words may be used to form new sentences:

NOUNS — claim, clothes, clew, cloud, claw, clerk, clove, globe, glue, cloak, gloom, clover, clause.

VERBS — glow, climb, close.

ADJECTIVES OR ADVERBS — close, gloomy, closely.

C — Exercise Story

Have you read the letter? story? poem?
Have you read the poem in the magazine?
Who wrote the poem?
Who is the author of the poem?
What is the name of the author?
How do you like the poem?
Have you read other poems by the same author?
He was a celebrated author.
He was a celebrated English author.
Johnson was a celebrated English author.
When did he live?
Can you tell me what he wrote?
One day......
One day a young lady came to Johnson.
One day a young lady came to Johnson to ask his advice.
One day a young lady came to Johnson to ask his opinion.
She gave Johnson a poem.
She gave him a poem to read.
She gave him a poem to read that she herself had written.

She gave him the poem and asked him to read it through and tell her what he thought of it.

What do you think of it?
How do you like it?
What is your opinion of this poem?
Give me your opinion? advice?

The young lady said to Johnson, "Give me your opinion of this poem?"

I have written more poems.
I have written other things.
I have written several other things.
I have planned to write more.
I have more irons in the fire.

One day a young lady came to Johnson, the celebrated author, and handing him a poem, asked him to please read it over and tell her what he thought of it, adding that she had more irons in the fire.

Johnson took the manuscript.
He took the manuscript and looked it over.
He glanced at the poem.
He read it through.
After reading through the poem,......
After reading through the poem, Johnson gave it back to the young lady.

After reading through the manuscript, Johnson gave it back to the young lady, and said; — remarked,......

As he handed it back to the young lady, he said, "I advise you to put this manuscript with your other irons in the fire."

JOHNSON AND THE AUTHOR

One day a young lady came to Johnson, the celebrated author, and, handing him a poem, asked him to read it over and tell her what he thought of it, adding that she had more irons in the fire.

"If that is so," said Johnson, looking over the manuscript, "I advise you to put these verses with your other irons in the fire."

LESSON XII

A

I. **n** before a vowel.

In **n** the point of the tongue is placed behind the upper gum. The teeth are only slightly separated, — the degree of opening depending upon the vowel that follows. There is only a very slight visible outward movement. It is very similar in appearance to **t** and **d,** but these have more jaw movement and are shorter.

Note. Do not spend too much time in trying to distinguish the **n** in a syllable. It is far better to practice **n, t** and **d** in short sentences.

II. Mirror Practice on Sounds.

1. Repeat rapidly in one breath:

nänänä — cä
nōnonō — cō
nānānā — cā

Notice that for both **n** and **c** the mouth is open. For **n** we see the tongue move, while in **k** (or hard **c**) there is more jaw movement.

2. Pronounce rapidly: —

the **cä** — the **nä**
the **cō** — the **nō**
the **cōō** — the **nōō**
the **cā** — the **nā**
the **kē** — the **nē**
the **kī** — the **nī**
the **cöw** — the **nöw**
the **cöĭ** — the **nöĭ**
the **cür** — the **nër**

Notice the same movements as in the preceding exercise.

3. Further comparisons: —

fä‿cä	**sō‿cä**	**mā‿cō**
fä‿nä	**sō‿nä**	**mā‿nō**
fā‿cā	**sō‿kī**	**mā‿cür**
fā‿nā	**sō‿nī**	**mā‿nür**

4. Syllable drills leading to sentences.

mā nō	**She may know the name.**
mā nā	**You may name them.**
mā nē	**We may need more.**
sō nē	**It is so near by.**
sō noi	**The boys are so noisy.**
mi nō	**My note was received.**
mi nur	**My nurse is neat.**
mi nā	**My name is Nora.**
mi nōō	**My new knife is sharp.**

B

I. Sentence Practice.

(a) I know them.
I know him.
I know him by sight.
I know him well.
Do you know who she is?
Do you know how she is?
Do you know how old he is?
Can you tell me his name?
I don't know.
How do you know?
Do you know how?
Do you know why?
Do you know why they came?
Do you know how to do that?
I know nothing about it.

I know them.
Do you think he knows about it?
I am afraid he knows nothing about it.
He must have known about it.
He must have known them.
I should be glad to know them.
I should be glad to know about it.
I will let them know.
Let me know.
Let me know by tomorrow.
Let me know when they come.
Let me know as soon as possible.
She said she would let me know as soon as possible.
If possible let me know by tomorrow.
He knew them.
He knew about it.
He knew that it was so.
I knew that it was nearby.
I knew the name.
I knew the number.
He told me that he knew nothing about it.

(b) What is the name of the flower?
What is the name of the street?
What is the name of the club?
What is the name of the ship?
What is the name of your niece?
What is the name of your nephew?
Do you know my nephew's name?
Perhaps he knows my nephew.
Perhaps he knows my niece.
My niece knew nothing about it.
My niece has heard the news.
I have had news from my niece.
We have had no news from them since November.
No news is good news.
They will arrive on the ninth of November.
What is your number? We have a new number.
Do you remember their number?
I remember the name but not the number.

Was it number nine?
Do you hear the noise?
The boys are very noisy.
There were nine boys in the class.
The nine boys belong to the same club.
Where is my knife?
I have a new knife.
I bought a new knife for my nephew.
Who is your neighbor?
What is your neighbor's name?
Do you know your neighbor?
Our neighbors have moved into their new house.
Have you anything new?
Show me your new knife.
Have you read the news?
What newspaper do you read?
My nephew brought home a newspaper at noon.
He comes home at noon.
Now I know how.
Now I know the way.
Now I know the name of the flower.

(c) Now or never......
Now we know.
Now we have none.
Now it is too late.
Now the time has come.
I knew that it was so.
I knew that it was nice.
I knew that it was nearby.
I knew that she was your niece.
I knew that the news had come.
I knew that the number had been changed.
Did you notice the number?
Did you notice the name?
Did you read the notice?
I read the notice in the newspaper.
There is nothing new in the newspaper.
We have nothing to read.
There is nothing to do to-night.

Nothing is known about it.
He said he knew nothing about it.
They must have known the name.
Neither one nor the other......
Neither now nor later......
Neither in the present nor in the future......
Neither today nor tomorrow......
Neither here nor there......
No one knew about it.
We have no hope.
There is no time like the present.
No one knew the new number.
There was no need of that.

(d) Do you know the number of their room?
Is it number nine or nineteen?
My father's office is on the ninth floor in the new building on North Street.
Do you need anything more before you go?
Are your new clothes warm enough?
You will need more new clothes if you go South.
Did you receive a note?
Give me the note that he brought you to-night.
Let me see your new note-paper.
I bought some new blue note-paper.
I must remember to write a note to my niece.
The next time you come you must bring your note-book.
Did you notice the name on the note-book?
Please let me read over your notes.
Did you notice how it was made?
Did you receive a notice from the club?
I notice that the name of the street has been changed.
We must notify them of the change.
Neither of them knew anything about it.
Did you speak to the nurse?
The new nurse is very neat.
They must have a new nurse for him.
Can you knit?
Will you show me how to knit the shawl?

My niece can neither knit nor crochet.
Will you buy some nuts for me?
I am fond of walnuts.
Who will crack some nuts for me?
That is a hard nut to crack.

II. Vocabulary.

These words may be used to form new sentences:

NOUNS — name, niece, nephew, noun, note, November, news, knife, newspaper, noon, knee, negro, neighbor, Norway, needle, night, nurse, nerve, noise, nose.

VERBS — know, knew, gnaw.

ADJECTIVES OR ADVERBS — neat, now, new, nine, neither, nor, nice, near.

C — Exercise Story

Shall I tell you a story?
Would you like to have me tell you a story?
The story is about an Englishman.
The story is about Lord Russell.
Lord Russell was a famous man.
He was a great man.
He was a great statesman.
He was a great diplomat.
Lord Russell went to Germany.
Lord Russell went to live in Germany.
Lord Russell was sent to live in Germany.
Lord Russell was sent to the Emperor of Germany.
Lord Russell was sent to the Court of the German Emperor.
Lord Russell was sent to the German Court.
He was an ambassador.
He was the English ambassador.
He was the English ambassador at the German Court.

The following story is told about a famous Englishman who was sent to the German Court at Berlin as ambassador.

One day......
One day he went to call upon someone.
One day he went to visit Prince Bismarck.
One day he went to make a call upon Bismarck.
They talked together for some time.
They had a long conversation together.
After a long conversation......
After they had been talking together for a long time......
Lord Russell said to Bismarck,......
Lord Russell remarked,......
"I suppose people often come to see you."
"I suppose people often annoy you with their visits."
"I presume you are often annoyed by tiresome visitors."
"Of course, a man like you is often annoyed by the visit of tiresome people."

When Lord Russell was the English ambassador at the German Court, he was one day making a call upon Prince Bismarck, and after rather a long conversation he remarked that the visits of tiresome people doubtless often annoyed a man like Bismarck.

"Have you ever thought of a way?"
"Have you ever thought of a way to get rid of them?"
"Have you ever thought of a way to rid yourself of them?"
"Surely there is a way."
"Surely you can find a way."
"Surely you can find some means to get rid of them."
"I suppose you have some means to get rid of them."
"Doubtless you have found some means to get rid of them."
"But you can surely get rid of such people by some means or other," said Lord Russell.

"Oh, yes," replied Bismarck.
"Oh, surely," said Bismarck.
"Of course I have a way," replied Bismarck.
"I have several ways,"......
"One way,"......
"One way, for instance,".....
"For example, my wife comes in,"......
"For example, my wife sometimes comes in,"........
"I have my wife come in," ....
"I have my wife come in and call me out for some reason,"....

"She calls me out for some reason or other,".......

"She calls me out on some pretext or another,"........

"And then — after that,"........

"And then after that the visitor has to leave,"......

"And then, of course, the visitor is obliged to leave,"......

"Of course," said Bismarck, "for example, I often have my wife come and call me out on one pretext or another, and then the visitor is obliged to leave."

He had scarcely spoken,....

Scarcely had he spoken,......

Scarcely had he spoken these words,......

Scarcely had he spoken these words when someone came in.

Someone entered.

Someone entered the room.

It was his wife.

She said to him — told him — remarked.

She remarked that it was time.

She remarked that it was time for him to take his medicine.

It was his wife who told him that it was time for him to take his medicine.

Bismarck had hardly spoken these words when the door opened and someone entered the room. It was his wife who told him that it was time for him to take his medicine.

Lord Russell was a man of the world.

He had a sense of humor.

He had a keen sense of humor.

He saw how funny it was.

He saw the funny side of it.

He saw the funny side of the affair.

Lord Russell, who had a keen sense of humor, saw the funny side of the affair.

He laughed.

He laughed aloud.

He laughed aloud at these words.

He burst out laughing at these words.

Then he took up his hat.

Then he took up his hat and left.

Lord Russell was so amused, he burst out laughing. Then he took up his hat and left.

RUSSELL AND BISMARCK

When Lord Russell was the English Ambassador at the German court, he went to call on Prince Bismarck one day. After a long conversation, he remarked that the visits of tiresome people doubtless often annoyed a man like the imperial chancellor.

"But you can surely get rid of such people by some means or other," continued Lord Russell.

"Of course," said Bismarck; "for example, I often have my wife come and call me out on one pretext or another, and then the visitors have to leave."

Scarcely had Bismarck spoken these words when someone entered. It was his wife, who said to him that it was time for him to take his medicine. Lord Russell, who was a man of the world, saw the humorous side of the affair, and broke out into a loud laugh at these words. Then he took his hat and left.

LESSON XIII

A

I. Short vowels.

Thus far we have practiced only the long vowels and the diphthongs. In this lesson we practice five short vowels, — **ă, ŏ, ĭ, ŭ, ĕ.**

1. In **ă** we see a slight downward movement of the jaw.

2. In **ŏ** we see a forward movement of the lips, — less round than for **âw.**

3. In **ĭ** we see a slight backward movement of the lips, — like **ē,** only shorter.

4. In **ŭ** we see a short downward movement, — like **ä,** only shorter.

5. In **ĕ** we see a shorter downward movement than for **ă.** The mouth does not open quite so wide. There is also a slight backward movement of the lower lip.

Note. We practice these vowels in combinations that occur most frequently in words.

II. Mirror Practice on Sounds.

1. Difference between **ă, ŏ, ĭ, ŭ, ĕ** followed by **n:** —

Note. In this exercise, pay less attention to the final consonants than to the vowel and the consonant that precedes.

ăn	**ŏn**	**ĭn**	**ŭn**	**ĕn**
băn	bŏn	bĭn	bŭn	bĕn
măn	mŏn	mĭn	mŭn	mĕn
păn	pŏn	pĭn	pŭn	pĕn
căn	cŏn	cĭn	cŭn	cĕn
făn	fŏn	fĭn	fŭn	fĕn
dăn	dŏn	dĭn	dŭn	dĕn
hăn	hŏn	hĭn	hŭn	hĕn
lăn	lŏn	lĭn	lŭn	lĕn
răn	rŏn	rĭn	rŭn	rĕn
săn	sŏn	sĭn	sŭn	sĕn
shăn	shŏn	shĭn	shŭn	shĕn
thăn	thŏn	thĭn	thŭn	thĕn
flăn	——	flĭn	——	——
slăn	——	——	——	slĕn
blăn	blŏn	blĭn	blŭn	blĕn
plăn	——	——	plŭn	plĕn
clăn	clŏn	clĭn	clŭn	clĕn
crăn	crŏn	crĭn	crŭn	——
brăn	brŏn	brĭn	——	——
prăn	——	prĭn	——	prĕn

2. Compare short vowels followed by **n** with the same short vowels followed by consonants of Class **I:** —

ăn‿ăf	**ăn‿ăs**	**ăn‿ăp**
ŏn‿ŏf	**ŏn‿ŏs**	**ŏn‿ŏp**
ĭn‿ĭf	**ĭn‿ĭs**	**ĭn‿ĭp**
ŭn‿ŭf	**ŭn‿ŭs**	**ŭn‿ŭp**
ĕn‿ĕf	**ĕn‿ĕs**	**ĕn‿ĕp**

B

I. Sentence Practice.

(a) Who is that man?
An old man came to our door.
Where is my fan?
My fan came from Japan.
Where is Japan?

The man brought me the fan from Japan.
What is in that can?
Can you tell me that man's name?
The man ran for the car.
We have a new plan.
What is your plan?
We plan to go to the sea-shore.
They plan to go to Japan.
Can you come?
Come as soon as you can.
They ran away.
Of course I will come as soon as I can.

On the farm....	On the half hour....
On the car....	On this....
On the way....	On that....
On the road....	On the other one....
On the river....	On the paper....
On the roof....	On the sign....
On the floor....	On the house....
On the hour....	On the cover of the book....

NOTE. As an exception, phrases are given in this lesson in connection with the sentence practice.

(b)	In the way....	In the right....
	In my way....	In the wrong way....
	In the South....	In bloom....
	In halves....	In May....
	In the book....	In my place....
	In a few months...	In your place....
	In a few years....	In the rain....
	In a year from now....	

The work was all in vain.
My rose-bush is in bloom.
You must do it in the right way.
Give me a pin.

Did you buy that pin in Japan?
I bought the pin in Berlin.
Where is the inn?
We were on the way to the inn.
The inn is on the same road.
What is the name of the inn?
Do you know the name of the inn in Lynn?

(c) Where is the other one?
Which one will you have?
There is only one....
One by one....
One after another....
One more....
I have only one.
Who won?
My brother won the game.
Where is your son?
They have one son.
Run away.
Run away now.
Run as far as you can.
He was run over.
What have you done?
What have you done with my fan?
It was done in fun.
How was it done?
Which one?
This one.
That one.
No, not that one.
I will have this one.
You may have that one.
May I keep this one?
You may keep whichever one you please.
Which one shall I keep?
Which one shall I give away?
Give him this one.
Please give me another one.
Please buy one for me.

I will buy one on the way.
That is in my way.
It must be done in the same way.
What can we do about it?
What can be done about it?
Nothing can be done about it now.

(d) When can you come?
When did you see the men?
We saw ten men.
I can't find my pen.
You must come then.
Come at ten if you can.
The wren is a bird.
I saw the wren.
I found my pen.
She gave me her pen.
Lend me your pen.
When will you come to see me?
My brother's name is Ben.
If I were in your place I should go then.
Shall we go to San Francisco?
She gave me the pen when we were in San Francisco.
We may go to Berlin in May.
My nephew is in Japan now.
I will go then if I can.
There were ten men in the boat.
We met the man at the inn.
What is the name of the man who keeps the inn?
Can you tell me if this is the right way to the inn?
We hope to return home in an hour and a half.
Then come tomorrow if you can.

II. Vocabulary.

Use these words to form new sentences:

NOUNS — man, pan, fan, clan, bin, pin, sin, kin, fin, Lynn, shin, bun, pun, fun, son, sun, men, pen, den, hen, wren, plan.

VERBS — run, ran, don, sun, shun, pin, sin, plan, win, won.

ADJECTIVES OR ADVERBS — thin, then, when, one.

C — Exercise Story

Have you heard the news?
Have you read the newspaper?
What paper do you read?
I read the advertisement in the paper.
I read it in the morning paper.
I read the announcement in the evening paper.
What did you read in the newspaper this morning?
The advertisement was in the morning paper.
The advertisement appeared in several of the newspapers.
One day an advertisement appeared in the paper.
One day a gentleman put an advertisment into the paper.
He advertised for a coachman.
An old gentleman advertised for a coachman.
Who answered the advertisement?
Who called at the house in reply to the advertisement?
Three men came.
Three men came to the gentleman's house.
They all came at the same time.
They all came on the same day.
The old gentleman talked with each of them.
He asked each one the same question.

He said, "How near can you drive to the edge of a precipice without going over?"

The first man said, "Within an inch."

The first man was sure that he could drive to within an inch of the precipice without going over.

The second man was asked the same question.

When the second man was asked the same question, he replied, "Within half an inch."

He said,"'I can drive within half an inch of a precipice. I have often done so."

The second man said, "Oh, I have often driven within half an inch of the edge of a precipice without going over."

Then the old gentleman asked the third man the same question.

This man replied, "I have never tried it, sir, and I am not sure that I should care to do so."

This reply pleased the old gentleman.

He engaged this man.

He immediately engaged this man.

He was always well satisfied with his choice.

He never had any reason to be sorry for his choice.

THE THREE COACHMEN

An advertisement had appeared in the papers which stated that an elderly gentleman wanted a coachman. Three men came on the same day to his house to apply for the situation.

He had them brought in, one by one, to his room, and asked each of them the same question: "How near can you drive to the edge of a precipice without going over?"

The first man said, "Within an inch."

"Very well," said the old gentleman, "you can go now, and I shall let you know whether I want you or not."

The second man was now called in, and he said he could drive within half an inch of the edge, and, in fact, had done it more than once.

He was then dismissed as the first had been, and the third man was called in. "Well, my man, and how near can you drive to the edge of a precipice?"

"Indeed, your honor, I never tried, and I'm not sure that I should care to."

"Ah," said the old gentleman, "you're the sort of man I want; now, what are your wages?"

The man told him and the gentleman engaged him at once. He never had any reason to be sorry for the choice he made.

LESSON XIV

A

I. **Long vowels** and **diphthongs** followed by **n:** — **ärn, ōwn** or **ōne** (as in **lōne**), **ōōn, ēēn, īne, öûn, ürn, öĭn.**

Note. A careful study of the above syllables will show that they are simply new combinations of letters previously studied. For example, **ärn** is a combination of **ä** in Lesson **I** and **n** in Lesson **XIII.**

II. Mirror Practice on Sounds.

1. In this exercise, pay less attention to the final consonant than to the vowel and consonants that precede.

ärn	**ōwn**	**ōōn**	**āin**	**ēēn**	**īne**	**öûn**	**ürn**
bärn	bōne	bōōn	bāne	bēan	bīne	böûn	bürn
märn	mōan	mōōn	māne	mēan	mīne	möûn	kërn
pärn	pōne	pōōn	pāne	kēēn	pīne	pöûn	fërn
därn	cōne	cōōn	cāne	dēan	kīne	göŵn	lëarn
färn	dōne	dōōn	dāne	lēan	dīne	döŵn	türn
lärn	fōne	fōōn	fāne	sēēn	fīne	föûn	
särn	hōne	lōōn	rāin	clēan	līne	löûn	
tärn	rōne	nōōn	sāne	grēēn	rīne	röûn	
värn	sōn	rōōn	slāin		sīgn	söûn	
	tōne	sōōn	plāne		blīne	töŵn	
	flōwn	tōōn	grāin		clīne	flöûn	
	blōwn	prōōn	frāin		brīne	blōûn	**öĭn**
	clōne	clōōn	brāin			clöŵn	cöĭn
	crōne					fröŵn	löĭn
	prōne					bröŵn	jöĭn

2. Compare long vowels and diphthongs followed by **n** with long vowels and diphthongs followed by consonants of Class **I.**

ärn‿ärve	**ärn‿ärce**	**ärn‿ärp**
ōne‿ōve	**ōne‿ōse**	**ōne‿ōpe**
ōōn‿ōōve	**ōōn‿ōōse**	**ōōn‿ōōp**
āin‿āve	**āin‿āce**	**āin‿āpe**
ēēn‿ēave	**ēēn‿ēase**	**ēēn‿ēēp**
īne‿īve	**īne‿īce**	**īne‿īpe**
ürn‿ürve	**ürn‿ürce**	**ürn‿ürp**

B

I. Sentence Practice.

(a) Do you own that barn?
The house and the barn belong to my father.
That is my own.
I am going there alone.
He came home alone.
We heard the man moan.
Give the dog a bone.
Can you make a corn-pone?
I found the pine-cone in the woods.
Show me the cone.
The sun shone all day.
How the boy has grown!
My niece has grown very tall.
The bluebird has flown away.
The birds have flown South.
She must have thrown the paper away.
How long has George V been on the throne?
He was thrown from his horse.
I hope it has not been thrown away.
Where is the river Rhone?
The name is well-known.
That man is a well-known writer.

If I had known about it then, I should have gone.
Can you hear over the 'phone?
Have you a telephone?

(b) Will you come soon?
Will you come at noon?
I shall go as soon as I can.
Have you seen the new moon?
We shall have to go before noon.
My brother comes home at noon.
I prefer to go in the afternoon.
The man will prune the rose-bush.
Have you ever seen a coon?
Can you play a tune on the piano?
The piano is out of tune.
I am afraid it will rain this afternoon.
We were in Maine this summer.
My wife spent the summer in Maine.
They live on Main Street.
That is the main street.
The man has bought a new cane.
Can you tell me how much he paid for his cane?
Does your father carry a cane?
The boy broke a pane of glass.
We had a fine crop of grain.
What kind of grain do they raise on their farm?
The work was all in vain.
He will gain nothing by that.
I saw a crane in the water.
The crane is a large bird.

(c) What do you mean by that?
I mean what I say.
Have you seen him?
I mean to go very soon.
I thought that you had seen them.
We saw only the first scene of the play.
The grass will soon be green.
The woman wore a green gown.
I prefer the green one.

Tell us what you have seen.
I think I have seen them.
Do you mean to say that I must go alone?
Do you really mean that?
Their house is so clean.
I have been down-town.
I mean to go down-town this afternoon.
I mean to ask her if she has seen them.
Can you come to town with us?
I cannot go now, but I will join you later.
They will spend the winter abroad, and we shall join them in the Spring.
We should be pleased to have you join us.
The cover of the book is brown.
How much is half a crown?
The crown of my hat is too high.
The bean is a vegetable.

(d) How much did he earn?
Do you think he can earn as much as that?
He did not learn his lesson well.
I am sure she cannot learn this.
Learn it by heart.
Learn to read.
Learn to speak French.
Learn to read the lips.
Learn your lesson.
Learn it over again.
Have you seen my fern?
Now it is my turn.
Burn the paper.
How did you burn yourself?
Be careful not to burn yourself.
You must return the book.
If you do not return the book by this afternoon you will have to pay a fine.
That is fine.
That would be a fine plan.
What is the name of the vine that grows on your house?
Have you a grape vine?

Will you have a glass of wine?
What kind of wine is this?
Is this Rhine wine?
Can you draw a straight line?
Write the word on the same line.
What does it say on that sign?
The man put up a large sign.
Did you sign your name to the paper?
There was no sign of rain when we left home.
That is mine.
No, that is not mine.
Give me the coin.
Where did you get that coin?

II. Vocabulary.

Use these words to form new sentences:

NOUNS — barn, bone, cone, 'phone, moon, coon, noon, mane, pain, pane, rain, plain, grain, brain, pine, line, sign, gown, town, clown, frown, burn, fern, turn, coin.

VERBS — darn, moan, rain, pine, dine, sign, frown, burn, learn, turn.

ADJECTIVES — prone, sane, plain, mine, fine, brown.

C — Exercise Story

Do you like to read?
What books are you reading?
I am reading an interesting story.
I have a very interesting (good) book.
Do you know the name of this book?
Do you want to know the name of this book?
It has a girl's name.
The girl lived on a farm.
The girl's name is "Rebecca."
The girl lived at Sunnybrook Farm.

The name of the book is "Rebecca of Sunnybrook Farm."
Do you know who wrote the book?
Do you know the name of the author?
The author is Kate Douglas Wiggin.
One evening the author was reading from her book.
She was reading to a number of people.
She was reading from "Rebecca."
She was reading from "Rebecca" to a large audience.
Many people were present.
Many people had come to hear Mrs. Wiggin read.
When the reading was over....
When the reading was finished.......
When the reading was finished, many people spoke to her.

When the reading was over, an old farmer went up to speak to Mrs. Wiggin.

The old man looked very shabby.
The old man had very poor clothes on.
The old man wore no collar and looked very shabby.

One evening, when Kate Douglas Wiggin, the author of "Rebecca of Sunnybrook Farm," had finished reading from one of her books to a large audience, an old farmer, very shabbily dressed, went up to speak to her.

What did the old man say?
What did the old man say to Mrs. Wiggin?
The old man said, "I have come a long way."
The old man said, "I have come a long way to hear you read."
The old man said, "I have come forty miles to hear you read."
Mrs. Wiggin was very much pleased.
Mrs. Wiggin was very glad.
Mrs. Wiggin was very happy.
The author smiled, she was very happy.
The old man said....continued....
The old man said, "I can't read much."
The old man said, "I can't read any real good stories."
The old man said, "I can't read what you call real good books."
He said, "I can't read anything that amounts to much."
"I am what you call an ignorant man."

"I am what you call an ignorant man for your books are about the only books I can read."

The old man said to her, "I have come forty miles to hear you read." The author was much pleased to hear this. The farmer continued, "Yes, I'm not a reading man at all. The fact is, I can't read anything that is what you call real good, or amounts to much; I am what you would call an ignorant man, for your books are about the only books that I can read."

THE ONLY BOOKS HE COULD READ

One evening, Kate Douglas Wiggin, the author of "Rebecca," was giving a reading from her works. After the reading was over an old man approached the author. He wore no collar, his trousers were very short, and every indication told of the " 'way back farmer."

He said to Mrs. Wiggin, "I've come forty miles to hear you read."

The author was very much pleased to hear this.

The old man continued, "Yes, I'm not a reading man at all. Fact is, I can't read anything that is what you call real good, or amounts to much. I'm what you would call an ignorant man, for your books are about the only ones I can read."

LESSON XV

A

I. **t** or **ed** at the end of a word after consonants of Class **I.**

ft, ved, st, pt (mt or **bt).**

There is a downward movement of the jaw when **t** or **ed** follow these consonants.

II. Mirror Practice on Sounds.

1. Difference between: —

ăf‿ăft	**ärve‿ärved**
ŏf‿ŏft	**ōōve‿ōōved**
ŭf‿ŭft	**āve‿āved**
ĭf‿ĭft	**ēave‿ēaved**
ĕf‿ĕft	**ürve‿ürved**

Notice that in **af** the mouth is closed at the end of the syllable by bringing the lower lip against the upper teeth. In **aft** it is opened when the **t** (or **ed**) is pronounced. Hence the downward movement.

2. Difference between: —

ăs‿ăst	**ōas‿ōast**
ŏs‿ŏst	**ōōs‿ōōst**
ŭs‿ŭst	**āze‿āzed**
ĭs‿ĭst	**ēas‿ēast**
ĕs‿ĕst	**ōĭs‿ōĭst**
	ürs‿ürst

Notice that in **as** the mouth is closed at the end of the syllable by bringing the teeth apparently together. In **ast** it is opened when the **t** (or **ed**) is pronounced.

3. Difference between: —

ăp‿ăpt	**ärm‿ärmed**
ŏp‿ŏpt	**ōpe‿ōped**
ŭp‿ŭpt	**ōōpe‿ōōped**
ĭp‿ĭpt	**āim‿āimed**
ĕp‿ĕpt	**ēam‿ēamed**
	ōrme‿ōrmed

Note. In the above syllables, it was necessary to use both **p** and **m** in order to bring in all combinations.

In this lesson, as in the two preceding ones, it is not wise to practice the syllables too much for the sake of seeing the final consonants. In rapid conversation they are not often seen, and it is far more important to get the right vowel and the preceding consonant.

B

I. Sentence Practice.

(a) They have left.
They have moved.
They have improved.
They have saved.
They have stopped on the way.
They have kept it.
He kept the book.
He hoped to go with them.
He left early.
He left in a hurry.
He had left it at home.
It was left here this morning.
How much have you left?

This is the last one.
This is the last one I have.
Perhaps this is the last one I have.
This may be the last one.
This is the last one there is.
This is the last one of all.
This is the last time.
This will be the last time.
How much will it cost?
What is the cost?
What have you lost?
I lost it.
I have lost it.
She lost her way.
She lost it on the way.
She is sure that she lost it on the way.
He lost it last evening.
He lost it the last time he was here.
I saw him the last time he was here.
It was the time before last.
It was the week before last that he was there.
It was the week before last that I saw him.

(b) They promised.
They must have promised.
They must have promised to come.
They must have passed the house.
They must have removed the sign.
They must have received the note.
They must have believed the story.
They must have improved.
They must have moved away.
They must have helped him.
They must have kept the key.
They must have left this morning.
They must have slept.
Perhaps she slept.
Perhaps she rapped on the door.
Whenever she rapped on the door.
Whenever she stopped on the way.

Probably he stopped on the way.
I wish that we had saved some of it.
How much have you saved?
The ship was saved.
The crew was saved when the ship sank.
Most of them were saved.
The street has been paved.
He paved the way for us.
They waved to us from the pier.
I hope that the boy behaved.
We passed them on the way.
It was half past four when they came.
You must not boast.
Will you have some toast?
It was the first time that he was here.
They missed the first train.
He was the first one to go.
This is the worst storm that we have had.

(c) Have you seen the raft in the river?
What a fine raft!
The boys have made a raft.
Please lift up the book for me.
The shaft is broken.
Did you sift the flour?
Be sure to sift the flour when you make the cake.
How much money have you left?
How many were left?
I have four books left.
Can you write with your left hand?
I carved the frame for you.
Who carved it?
I believe they have moved South.
The clock is fast.
My clock is always fast.
You must walk very fast.
Did you come on the fast train?
The ship has a high mast.
We passed a ship with a high mast.

Have you ever been West?
Who is going East with you this summer?
They came East last winter.
East or West, home is best.
Last, but not least.
We missed the fast train.
That is the best way.
It must be the best way.
That is too soft.
The boys are playing in the hay-loft.
She coughed all night.

(d) What have you lost?
I have lost my list.
My brother's name was last on the list.
Her name was first on the list.
Have you made out a list for me?
Put my name on the list.
This list is too long.
The last list was lost.
Please get me another list.
She slipped on the floor and broke her wrist.
Do you play whist?
Let us have a game of whist.
I sprained my wrist.
Must you go?
Must he go West now?
It must be done by tomorrow.
The list must be ready by the first of the week.
It must have cost more.
Someone rapped on the door.
I wrapped the book in brown paper.
He is very apt to come at this time.
They are not apt to be at home in the evening.
Give me the rest of it.
You may keep the rest of it.
It will be best to go on the fast train.
That is the best train.
The first train is the best one.

II. Vocabulary.

Use these words to form new sentences:

NOUNS — raft, shaft, gift, theft, mast, past, post, coast, feast, fist, whist, waist, harvest, list, nest, cost.

VERBS — lift, sift, paved, engraved, saved, waved, believed, grieved, moved, proved, curved, passed, roast, refused, invest, arrest, crossed, hoped, reaped, claimed, kept, whipped, stormed.

ADJECTIVES AND ADVERBS — swift, fast, last, east, west, best, pleased.

C — Exercise Story

There was once an artist....painter....famous artist.
There was once upon a time a celebrated artist.
This artist lived abroad....in Italy.
He had always lived in Italy. He was an Italian.
Have you ever been to Italy?
Do you know any Italian?
Have you ever met any Italian artists?
Can you tell me the names of three Italian artists?
Can you tell me who the most famous Italian artist was?
This story is about a celebrated Italian painter.
The painter had many pupils.
He had a large class of pupils.
Many pupils came to him.
Once upon a time there was a famous Italian painter who had a number of pupils who came to his studio every day.
Sometimes the painter left the pupils alone in his studio.
The pupils were left alone.
When the pupils were left alone,....
When the artist went out,....
When the artist went out and left his pupils alone,....
He left orders.
He left orders with his pupils.
He told the pupils what to do.

He told them what to do in case someone called.

He told them what to do in case someone called during his absence.

If someone called during his absence, they were told to write down the name.

They were told to write down the names of all visitors.

The artist told his pupils to be sure and write down the names of all the people who called.

One day the artist went out.

He went out one morning.

He went out one morning and left the pupils alone.

While he was away,.... During his absence....

During his absence, someone called.

Someone came to see the artist.

Someone came to the door and asked for the painter.

Three gentlemen came to the door.

They knocked at the painter's door.

The door was opened.

One of the pupils opened the door.

The door was opened immediately by one of the pupils.

Immediately one of the pupils went to the door.

One day the painter went out and left his studio in charge of his pupils who were told to open the door if someone knocked.

The gentlemen inquired for the artist.

"Is the artist at home?"

"Is Mr. So and So at home?"

"Can I see Mr. So and So?"

The pupil replied,....

The pupil who went to the door replied,....

The pupil who opened the door told the gentlemen that his teacher was not at home.

"I am sorry, but Mr. So and So has gone out."

"I cannot tell you when he will return."

"He will return before long."

The gentlemen, however, decided not to wait for him.

They went away.

They went away before the pupil remembered to ask their names.

The pupil forgot to ask the three gentlemen their names.

He forgot the instructions of the artist who had told him to be sure to write down the name of every person who called.

After a while....Later....Sometime afterwards....

A short time afterwards the painter returned.

He returned home. He returned to his studio.

When he returned to his studio,....

When he returned to his studio, he asked his pupils,....

He asked them....

He asked them if anyone had called.

"Has anyone been here this morning?" asked the painter of his pupils.

The pupil replied, "Oh, yes."

"Yes, sir," said the pupil.

"Yes, sir," said the pupil, "three gentlemen called."

"They wished very much to see you."

"They were very anxious to see you."

"They were disappointed not to find you at home."

A short time afterwards, when the painter returned and asked his pupils if anyone had called, he was much disappointed to find that three gentlemen had called during his absence.

He was disappointed.

He was still more disappointed....

He was still more angry....

He was still more angry when he heard that the pupil had forgotten to ask their names.

He scolded him severely.

The pupil made no reply.

The pupil said nothing.

The pupil said nothing but took a piece of paper and a pencil.

He took a piece of paper and a pencil in his hand.

He took a sheet of paper.

He took a sheet of paper and began to draw something.

He drew the picture of the three gentlemen.

He drew the picture of the three gentlemen so well....

The pupil made a rapid sketch of the visitors.

He made such a good sketch of the visitors that his teacher recognized them immediately.

He was so surprised.

He was so surprised when he saw the sketch.

He was delighted with the skill of his pupil.

THE ARTIST AND HIS PUPIL

Once upon a time there was a famous Italian painter, who had a number of pupils who came to his studio every day. Sometimes the artist left his pupils alone in his studio. They were told to write down the name of anyone who called during his absence.

One morning while the artist was out, three gentlemen called. The pupil who opened the door told the gentlemen that his teacher was not at home. They decided not to await his return. They left before the pupil remembered to ask their names.

A short time afterwards, when the painter returned and asked his pupils if anyone had called, he was much disappointed to find that three gentlemen had called. He scolded his pupil when he found that he had forgotten to ask their names.

The pupil said nothing, but took a sheet of paper and made such a good sketch of the visitors that his teacher recognized them immediately.

LESSON XVI

A

I. **t** or **ed** at the end of a word, after consonants of Class **II.**

rt and **lt** or **red** and **led.**

There is a slight upward movement of the jaw when **t** or **ed** follows **r** or **l.**

II. Mirror Practice.

1. Difference between: —

är‿är**t**	ȧir‿ȧir**ed**
ōr‿ōr**t**	ōar‿ōar**ed**
ür‿ür**t**	ēar‿ēar**ed**
	īre‿īr**ed**

Note. The upward movement is not very plain, since the mouth remains open while pronouncing the last sound.

2. Difference between: —

ăl‿ăl**t**	ōōl‿ōōl**ed**
ĕl‿ĕl**t**	ēēl‿ēēl**ed**
ĭl‿ĭl**t**	īle‿īl**ed**
ŭl‿ŭl**t**	ōŵl‿ōŵl**ed**
āil‿āil**ed**	ōĭl‿ōĭl**ed**
ōl‿ōl**ed**	ürl‿ürl**ed**

See note above.

Note. In this lesson spend more time in sentence practice under **B** than in syllable practice, since in rapid conversation final **t** or **ed** are seldom emphasized enough to be visible.

B

I. Sentence Practice.

(a) Have you learned your part?
My part is short.
I have read the first part.
Give me a part of it.
What time did you start?
You must start early.
Start at once.
Learn it by heart.
It is too hard.
The work was too hard for the boy.
They have had a hard time.
Where did you find that card?
Where did you board?
He will board with them this winter.
How much does he pay for his board?
The shoes must be repaired.
They have repaired the roof of the house.
Where is the fort?
I will show you the way to the fort.
It is only a short way from here to the fort.
What is the name of the fort?
Did you go on board the warship?
We met them on board the ship.
I feared that he would not come.

(b) Are you fond of art?
Have you been to the Art Museum?
I met her on the way to the Art Museum.
We have a fine new Art Museum.
My niece goes to the Art School.
Give me your chart.
That is a good chart.
How much did you pay for that chart?
I cannot afford to pay so much.

He cannot afford to pay so much for his board.
The ship has come into port.
Did you read the report in the newspaper?
The report was short.
What kind of a bird is that?
That is a robin-redbreast.
I saw a bluebird in the garden.
I have hurt my hand.
The boy was hurt by the automobile.
I am afraid it will hurt you.
Have you heard about it?
Have you heard how the man was hurt?
What is the word?
How do you spell that word?
What does that word mean?
That is the first time that I have seen that word.
They promised to send me word.
Who received the reward?
They offered a reward.
I heard that they had offered a reward.
Write your name on this card.
I found this card on the floor in the Art Museum.

(c) She has failed.
The ship sailed at four o'clock.
The letter was mailed.
It was sealed.
The house was sold.
He told me that the house was sold.
How old is your brother?
My father has sold the old house on the hill.
We have had very cold weather.
It is too cold to go out.
Are you cold?
Fold the paper.
What ailed her?
They felt that it would be the best way.
I felt sure that he would go.
It was my fault.
That is your own fault.

At first we were afraid that it was the boy's fault.
We felt very sorry for the boy.
They felt the cold.
The ice will soon melt.
Have you seen my new belt?
I bought a black belt.
The glass was filled to the brim.
It was filled with water.

(d) They failed to come on time.
I mailed the letter at the post-office.
The ship sailed at three o'clock on Friday.
They sailed from New York.
Have you sealed the letter?
Are you sure that you sealed it before you mailed it?
She wore a broad-brimmed hat to shield her eyes from the sun.
The farmer was in the corn-field.
We will cross the field on our way to the post-office.
Who owns that field?
How large is the field?
The vase was filled with flowers.
Who filled my fountain-pen?
I filled it for you this morning.
Who built this house?
It was built many years ago.
Shall you have that old picture framed?
I think I shall get a gilt frame.
They called for me on the way to the Art Museum.
How old is that man?
Fold the paper and put it into an envelope.
What is the best way to fold it?
The farmer has sold his farm and moved away.
The old place will be sold.
Who told you that it would be sold?

II. Vocabulary.

These words may be used to form new sentences:

NOUNS — art, part, cart, card, board, heart, reward, sport, port, court, cord, fort, report, word, shield, field, fault, malt, mould, gold, child.

VERBS — start, board, aired, cared, failed, mailed, sailed, nailed, sealed, filled, built, killed, fold, sold, scold, soiled, boiled, curled, furled, hurt.

ADJECTIVES — hard, gilt, cold, mild, wild, short, old, third.

C — Exercise Story

Have you been away?
Have you been away on the train?
How far did you go?
Do you like to travel?
Do you like to ride on the train?
Did you ever ride in an automobile?
Do you prefer to ride in a carriage?
Did you ever ride in an omnibus?
Do you often ride in a taxi-cab?
Did you ever ride in a hansom?
Did you ever ride in a hansom in New York?
Many people ride in hansoms in New York and London.
Did you ever ride on Fifth Avenue in a hansom?
Did you ever ride in a Fifth Avenue stage?
Did you ever ride on top of a Fifth Avenue stage-coach?
Did you ever ride in a stage-coach?
Did you ever see one of the old-fashioned stage-coaches?
A long time ago....
Many years ago, before the steam-engine was invented.....
Many years ago, before the invention of the steam-engine....
Before the invention of the steam-engine, everybody traveled in stage coaches.
It was not very comfortable riding in a stage coach.
It was not so comfortable in a stage-coach as it is on the train.

A stage-coach is not so comfortable as the train.

A stage-coach is not so comfortable as a Pullman car.

Traveling in a stage-coach was not very comfortable.

Traveling in a stage-coach was not very safe.

The roads were not very safe.

There were a great many thieves.

There were a great many robbers.

The stage-coaches were often robbed.

The stage-coaches were often held up.

The stage-coaches were often held up by highwaymen.

Once upon a time....

Once upon a time, some people were traveling.

Some people were traveling in a stage-coach.

Several people were traveling in a stage-coach.

Several people were traveling in a stage-coach from Liverpool to London.

There were several men in the stage-coach.

There were several men and one lady.

It was a very dark night.

The night was very dark.

The night was very dark, and the people were afraid.

They were afraid that they might be held up.

They were afraid that a highwayman might hold them up.

A highwayman might hold them up.

A highwayman might hold them up and take their money away from them.

They were afraid of losing their money.

They all had money with them.

One gentleman said that he had a great deal of money with him.

One gentleman said that he had ten pounds with him.

He had ten pounds with him, and he was afraid he might lose it.

He did not want to lose it.

He wanted to hide it.

He wanted to hide it where the highwayman could not find it.

He asked the other men where he should hide it.

He asked the lady where she thought he ought to hide it.

The lady told him to hide the money in his boots.

He had just put the money into his boots....

He had just put the money into his boots, when the coach stopped.

Someone stopped the coach.

A highwayman stopped the coach, and ordered the travelers to give him their money.

The lady who was in the coach....

The lady who was in the coach spoke to the highwayman.

The lady told the highwayman that she did not have any money.

The lady said, "I have no money, but that gentleman over there has ten pounds in his boots."

The gentleman was very much surprised.

The gentleman was very angry.

The gentleman was very angry, but he had to give up the money.

He had to give up the ten pounds.

The highwayman took the ten pounds, and went away.

After he had gone....

After he had gone, all the men in the coach began to talk to the lady.

They were all very angry.

They all talked at once.

They all said that the lady was to blame.

They all said that the lady was a thief.

They all said that the lady was a partner of the highwayman.

They accused the lady of being in partnership with the highwayman.

The lady said it was not true.

She said she would show them that it was not true.

She said she would prove to them that it was not true.

She asked them to come to her house.

She asked them to come to her house in London.

She asked them all to come and see her on the following day.

She asked them all to come to dinner on the following day.

She said that if they would all come to dinner at her house in London, on the following day, she would prove to them that she was not a thief.

The next day....

The next day, they all went to her house in London.

It was a very beautiful house.
It was a very large and beautiful house.
They had a fine dinner.
They had a magnificent dinner.
After dinner....
After dinner, the lady asked them all to come into the drawing room.
When they were all in the drawing-room, they saw....
They saw that the lady had something in her hand.
The lady had a pocket-book in her hand.
She gave it to the gentleman.
She gave it to the gentleman who had lost the ten pounds.
She gave it to him and said.
She said, "I am very sorry."
"I am very sorry that I had to do such a thing."
"I hope you will forgive me."
"I hope you will pardon me."
"I beg your pardon."
"I apologize."
"I apologize most sincerely."
"Please accept my apologies for what I did last night."
"I had to do it."
"There was nothing else for me to do."
"I could not do anything else."
"I could not do anything except to tell the highwayman where your money was."
"I had to tell him."
"If I had not told him he would not have gone away."
"I had a great deal of money with me."
"I had a thousand pounds with me."
"I had a thousand pounds with me, and I was afraid that he would find them."
"Here is your money."
"Here is fifty pounds for you."
"Here is fifty pounds to make up for the ten that you lost."
"You must take the money."
"You must accept the money."
"I think I am fortunate."
"I think I am very fortunate to save the thousand pounds."

"You must accept the money, for I consider myself very fortunate to have saved the thousand pounds."

The gentleman was very much pleased.

All the gentlemen were very much pleased.

They thought that the lady was very clever.

They thought that the lady was very clever, and also very generous.

They thought the lady was very clever as well as very generous.

THE STAGE COACH

Several years ago, some people were traveling in a stage-coach towards London. At the approach of night, they began to express their fears of being attacked by highwaymen. One gentleman said he had ten guineas, and did not know where to hide them for safety. A lady who sat next to him in the coach advised him to conceal them in his boots, which he immediately did. Soon after a highwayman came up and demanded their purses. The lady told him that she had no money, but that, if he would search that gentleman's boots, he would find ten guineas.

The astonished traveler was obliged to submit and lost his money, but, as soon as the robber was gone, he loaded the lady with abuse, declaring she was a confederate of the thief. She acknowledged that appearances were against her, but added that, if the travelers would all do her the honor to dine with her on the following day, she would explain to their satisfaction her conduct which appeared so mysterious.

They consented, and after partaking of a magnificent dinner, the lady took them into the drawing-room. There she showed them a pocket-book and said, "Here is an apology for my conduct of last night. It contains bank-notes for several hundred pounds." Then addressing herself to the gentleman she said: "Sir, if I had not directed the highwayman's attention to your ten guineas, I should have lost my bank-notes. I therefore beg that, to make you amends for your loss and vexation, you will accept one of these bank-notes for a hundred pounds. No excuses, sir, for I consider myself fortunate in saving the others at that price."

The travelers were highly pleased with the lady's generosity, and complimented her on her presence of mind.

LESSON XVII

A

I. d (or **t**)**, k,** and **g** after **n** preceded by a vowel.

Syllables are given here but it is not advisable to spend time in practising these before a mirror.

The difference is only slight. Syllables ending in **nd** (or **ned**)**, nk** (really ngk)**, ng** after a vowel are somewhat longer than those ending in **n.** There is some movement at the corners of the mouth and in the cheeks.

ăn‿ăn**d**	ōōn‿ōōn**ed**	ăn‿ăn**k**
ŏn‿ŏn**d**	ēēn‿ēēn**ed**	ŏn‿ŏn**g**
ĭn‿ĭnn**ed**	öûn‿öûn**ed**	ŭn‿ŭn**g**
ĕn‿ĕn**d**	īne‿īn**ed**	ĭn‿ĭn**k**
āin‿āin**ed**	öĭn‿öĭn**ed**	
ōwn‿ōwn**ed**	ürn‿ürn**ed**	

B

I. Sentence Practice.

(a) Send it to me.
Send it by mail.
Send for the book.
Send me a message.
Send a reply by the messenger.
Send it off immediately.
Send it back.
Send word to him at once.
Send him a message to the Art Club.
Shall I send it?
Who will send it?
Have you sent it?
You may send it.
You ought to send it to her.

Who sent the child there?
Will you please send me the book by to-morrow?
Why did n't you send me word?
Whe sent to the post-office for some stamps.
The letter was sent by Special Delivery.
The package was sent C. O. D.
It is not necessary to have it sent by mail.
The two registered letters were sent off at the same time.
Send it by freight.
Go to the post-office and send the letter at once.
She telephoned me that the flowers should be sent before nine o'clock.
Before you send off the report, make a copy of it.
I shall remember to send her the manuscript.
They have sent me four books instead of five.
Perhaps it was sent by mistake.
The message should be sent without delay.

(b) Think it over.
Think about it.
Think up something.
Think out a plan.
Think over the matter.
Think it all out.
Think seriously about it.
What have you found?
Have you found it out?
Can you find out about it?
It is hard to find out anything about it.
We found a part of it.
We sent part of it to you.
We meant to send it.
We meant to find out about it.
We meant to hunt for it.
They found fault with everything.
I thank you.
We must thank them for the flowers.
Lend me your book.
Please lend it to me for an hour.

When did you lend it to him?
Can you mend it for me?
Will you find it for me?
Hand it to me.
Hand me the book.
Will you send me the book when you find it?
If you think of it, ask her to lend me the book if she can find it.
Send her for it whenever you think of it.
Mend it before you send it.
If you wish to lend it to her, you must think to mend it before you send it.

(c) I have learned my lesson.
He has learned the poem by heart.
How much money has he earned?
The house was burned to the ground.
Who owned the barn that was burned?
Have the book bound.
It must be rebound.
Have you found out who bought the land?
I think I have found the right way.
What do you think of the plan?
I think it will come out right in the end.
Where did the ship sink?
The ship sank in the sound.
The bank has failed.
Lend me the new French novel?
Please go to the bank with me.
The tank was filled with water.
Can you hear the sound of my voice?
Will you have the coffee ground?
Grind it for me.
Ask the grocer to grind the coffee, and then send it to me.
I bought a pound of coffee.
We have planned to go South this winter.
They have raised a large fund.
How did the story end?
It rained from morning till night.

We should have gone to row on the pond it if had not rained.
Show us the way to the pond.

(d) If you think it will be all right, I will send it to them at once.
Do not go to the bank before they send you word.
I filled out the blank and sent it to the bank.
The story was very interesting from beginning to end.
I did not read the end of the story.
As soon as you are ready we will go to the bank.
What time do they close the bank?
Do you think that it is her fault that the book was not sent?
Do you use black ink?
What kind of ink do they use in the bank?
I prefer to write with blue ink.
Think it over before you make up your mind.
If you lose the book you will be fined.
He signed the paper at the bank.
Have you wound the clock?
My new table is round.
What have you in your hand?
Which one will you have, the pink one or the blue one?
I prefer the pink one.
Do you think that he earned the money?
I think he earned more than that.
The boys have planned to earn some money.
They earned the money for the fund.
I believe they have earned enough to buy the land.
They are bound to do it.

II. Vocabulary.

These words may be used to form new sentences:

NOUNS — hand, land, sand, band, bond, fund, pond, end, bank, blank, rank, pound, gong, rung, pung, ink, tank, pink, plank, crank.

VERBS — sinned, found, bound, owned, loaned, rained, gained, crowned, ground, planned, sank, think, sink, thank, send, lend, mend, hand, grind, fined, coined, earned, learned, burned.

ADJECTIVES — found, frank.

C — Exercise Story

Where have you been?
Have you been to the concert?
Have you been to the theatre?
Have you been to the lecture?
Where was the lecture?
Who was the lecturer?
What was the subject of the lecture?
It was an interesting lecture.
The lecture was too long.
Could you follow the lecturer?
Could you read the lecturer's lips?
Did you ever hear Mark Twain lecture?
Once Mark Twain gave a lecture in a small town.
Once Mark Twain went to a small town to give a lecture.
Before the lecture....
Before the lecture he went out.
Before the lecture he went into a barber-shop.
One day, Mark Twain arrived at a small town to give a lecture.
Before the lecture he went into a barber-shop to be shaved.
What did the barber say?
What did he say to Mark Twain?
The barber said to him, "Are you a stranger?"
Mark Twain replied, "Yes."
Mark Twain replied, "Yes, this is the first time I have been here."
When the barber asked Mark Twain if he were a stranger, he answered that he had never been in that town before.
The barber continued....
The barber continued to talk to the stranger.
Did he say anything about the lecture?

Did he tell the stranger anything about the lecture?

The barber said to the stranger, "Mark Twain is going to lecture here this evening."

Are you going?

Are you going to the lecture?

I suppose you will go.

I suppose you will go to hear him lecture.

I suppose you would like to go to the lecture.

Mark Twain replied, "Oh, I guess so."

Have you bought your ticket?

Where can I buy a ticket?

How much are the tickets?

How many tickets will you buy?

"Have you bought your ticket?" said the barber.

"No, not yet."

Mark Twain replied, "No, not yet."

How many tickets have been sold?

How many tickets to Mark Twain's lecture have been sold?

The barber told the stranger that every ticket had been sold.

"Everything is sold out," said the barber.

Did you ever have to stand during a lecture?

It is very tiresome to stand.

"How very annoying," said Mark Twain.

Mark Twain said with a sigh, "I never saw such luck?"

The barber told the stranger that everything was sold out and that he would have to stand.

Mark Twain replied, "How very annoying. I never saw such luck! I always have to stand when that fellow lectures."

MARK TWAIN'S HARD LUCK

In the course of his lecture trips, Mark Twain arrived at a small town. Before dinner he went into a barber-shop to be shaved. The barber said to him, "You are a stranger."

"Yes," replied Mark Twain.

"You chose a good time to come," said the barber. "Mark Twain is going to read and lecture here this evening. You'll go I suppose?"

"Oh, I guess so."

"Have you bought your ticket?"

"Not yet."

"But everything is sold out. You'll have to stand."

"How very annoying," said Mark Twain with a sigh. "I never saw such luck! I always have to stand when that fellow lectures."

LESSON XVIII

A

I. **s** at the end of a word after consonants of Class **I.**

fs (vs), ps, (ms or **bs).**

In pronouncing **s** after consonants of Class **I,** we see a downward movement of the lower lip.

II. Mirror Practice on Sounds.

1. Difference between: —

ăp‿ăp**s**	ärp‿ärp**s**
ŏp‿ŏp**s**	ōpe‿ōpe**s**
ĭp‿ĭp**s**	o͞op‿o͞op**s**
ŭp‿ŭp**s**	āpe‿āpe**s**
ĕp‿ĕp**s**	ēēp‿ēēp**s**
	īpe‿īpe**s**
	ürp‿ürp**s**

Notice that in **ăp** the lips are closed at the end of the syllable. When **s** follows **p,** we see a downward movement of the lower lip. This movement is necessary in order to emit the breath when **s** is pronounced. In **ms** and **bs** the movement is the same as in **ps.**

2. Difference between: —

ăf‿ăf**s**	ärve‿ärve**s**
ŏf‿ŏf**s**	ōve‿ōve**s**
ĭf‿ĭf**s**	o͞ove‿o͞ove**s**
ŭf‿ŭf**s**	āve‿āve**s**
	ēave‿ēave**s**
	īvē‿īve**s**
	ürve‿ürve**s**

In **fs** and **vs** we also see a downward movement of the lower lip. At the same time the lower teeth which were covered while pronouncing **f** or **v** are visible. The lower jaw does not move.

B

I. Sentence Practice.

(a) Where are my gloves?
Where are my caps?
Where are my wraps?
Where are my cups?
Where are my cuffs?
Where are my knives?
Where are my grapes?
Where are my plumes?
Where are my pipes?
Where are my maps?
These are the old maps.
Show me the new pipes.
I have bought some blue plumes.
Give me a bunch of grapes?
The new knives are very sharp.
What has become of my new cuffs?
Are your new cuffs blue?
When you go out put on your wraps.
The boys have some new caps.
I have lost a pair of gloves.
What kind of gloves shall I buy?
What kind of grapes do you like best?
The ships went ashore on the reefs.
The waves are very high after the storm.
I love to watch the waves.
He hopes to come.
She comes twice a week.
He believes the report.
He roams about the woods.

She keeps it to herself.
It gives her pleasure.
It gives us hope.
It gives us time.
It gives them a chance.
It gives them much pleasure.
It gives them something to talk about.
It gives them a new object in life.
It gives us a new point of view.
It gives us a clear idea.
It gives us the other side.
It gives us a good account of the play.
It seems to be true.
It seems to move.
It seems to grow.
It seems to renew their hopes.
It seems too bad.
It seems to be true.
It seems impossible.
Ir seems best.
It seems a long way.
It seems a long time.
It seems very hard.
It seems to be the same size.
It seems she keeps up.
It seems he gives up too soon.

(c) The water foams.
The ship moves.
The boy sleeps.
The man blames him.
He claims the watch.
He whips the horse.
He claps his hands.
He stops on the way.
He hopes to be here on time.
My father hopes to hear about it.
He believes that it is so.
As soon as he comes I shall let you know.
When she comes, ask her about it.

How many rooms are there in your new house?
What are the names of those two men?
Can you remember their names?
Have you heard the rhymes?
There are four sloops in the harbor.
I saw the sloops.
We saw some beautiful plumes in the shops.
All the best shops are on Main Street.
I bought these maps this morning.
Those maps belong to my brother.
He left his maps at home.
Do you like to draw maps?

(d) She hopes that you will come so that she may show you her new house.
She comes to town twice a week for her lesson.
He believes that the report is true.
If she keeps the book too long she will be fined.
It seems very hard at first.
This one seems to be much smaller than that one.
It seems to me that that would be the best way.
The man blames his son for the accident.
If she stops on the way she will not be here before noon.
She hopes to be here in time to go with me.
My father hopes to hear from them before tomorrow.
He believes that they arrived last week.
It seems that they have sent word to him to come home.
How many names were on the list?
The last list contained more names than the first one.
How many loaves of bread did you buy?
I bought two loaves of bread and some grapes.
I sent the grapes to my friend.
Do you remember the fable about the fox and the grapes?
The fox thought the grapes were too sour.
Which do you prefer, grapes or plums?
The plums are ripe now.
Bring me a pound of plums when you go to town.

He leaves town tomorrow.
If he leaves on the early train he will be here by noon.

II. Vocabulary.

These words may be used to form new sentences:

NOUNS — arms, farms, names, seams, brooms, groups, plumes, plums, sloops, caps, capes, gloves, maps, grapes, cuffs, knives, shelves, rooms.

VERBS — seems, comes, hopes, gives, lives, roams, keeps, foams.

C — Exercise Story

One morning....
Every morning....
Every morning I go down-town.
I go down town every morning on the car.
I go down town every morning on the street-car.
The street-cars are full of people.
In the morning the street-cars are full of people.
In the morning the street-cars are always crowded.
I sometimes have to stand up.
I almost always have to stand up.
The cars are always so crowded that I can never get a seat.
How much is the fare on the street-car?
Who takes up the fare on the street-car?
The conductor takes up the fare on the car.
The fare is five cents.
Give the conductor five cents.
I have no change.
Here is a fifty-cent piece.
Here is a five-dollar bill.
Ask the conductor if he can change a five-dollar bill.
The conductor took the money.
The conductor gave me the change.
The conductor rang the bell.

The conductor rang up the fare.
The conductor gave me a transfer.
Ask the conductor for a transfer.
Does this car go through the subway?
Is this a subway car?
We are on the wrong car.
We must get off at the transfer-station.
Please stop the car.
I want to get off.
When I came down town this morning, the car was not very crowded.
There were several men on the car.
There was one young man on the car.
A young man sat opposite me.
When the car stopped....
When the car stopped the young man got up.
He did not get off the car.
He walked to the end of the car.
He walked to the door of the car.
He saw something on the floor.
He stooped to pick up something.
He picked up something and looked at it.
He looked at it very closely.
He looked at it very carefully.
He looked at it carefully to see what it was.
It was a piece of money.
It was a coin.
He looked at the coin and said....
He remarked....
He spoke in a loud voice.
He asked loudly, "Has anyone lost anything?"
"Has anybody lost a five-dollar gold piece?"
There was another man on the car.
He was a tall man.
He was a very tall man.
He was a very tall man with a solemn face.
He was a solemn-faced man.
He was sitting at the other end of the car.
A solemn-faced man, who was sitting at the other end of the car got up.

He got up and said, "Yes."
"Yes, I have lost something."
"Yes, I have lost a five-dollar gold piece."
"That belongs to me."
"That is mine."
"That must be mine."
"That must be the one I lost."
He went up to the young man.
He went up the young man and held out his hand.
He went up to the young man and eagerly held out his hand.
He held out his hand eagerly for the coin.
The young man gave him the coin.
The young man put the coin into his hand.
The young man gave him the coin that he had found.
The young man said,....
The young man gave him the coin and remarked,....
"I am sorry for you."
"I feel very sorry for you."
"I feel very sorry for you that you have lost a five-dollar gold piece."
"I am very sorry for your loss."
"Here are five cents."
"Here is a five-cent piece to help make up for your loss."

STORY

One day, a young man, riding on the street-car, picked up a coin from the floor. He examined it carefully, and then called out in a loud voice, "Has anyone lost a five-dollar gold piece?"

Instantly a solemn-faced man at the other end of the car strode forward.

"Yes, I've lost a five-dollar gold piece," he said eagerly holding out his hand.

"Well," said the young man, giving him the coin, "I'm sorry for you. Here's five cents toward making good your loss."

LESSON XIX

A

I. **s** at the end of a word after consonants of Class **II.**

ks (or **gs**), **ds** (or **ts**), **ls**

In pronouncing **s** after consonants of Class **II,** we see an upward movement of the lower jaw.

II. Mirror Practice on Sounds.

1. Difference between: —

ăck‿ăck**s**	är**k**‿ärk**s**
ŏck‿ŏck**s**	ōak‿ōak**s**
ook‿ook**s**	āke‿āke**s**
ĕck‿ĕck**s**	ēēk‿ēēk**s**
ĭck‿ĭck**s**	īke‿īke**s**
	ūrk‿ūrke**s**

Notice in pronouncing **ăck** the mouth remains open, while in **ăcks** the teeth are brought together after pronouncing **k** and therefore we see an upward movement of the jaw.

Note. The letter **x** is pronounced like **ks** and therefore, words ending in **x** come under this group.

tă**cks** — tă**x**
flŏ**cks** — phlŏ**x**

2. Difference between: —

ăl‿ăls	**ärl‿ärls**	**īle‿īles**
ĕll‿ĕlls	**ōle‿ōles**	**ŏŵl‿ŏŵls**
ĭll‿ĭlls	**ōōl‿ōōls**	**ŏĭl‿ŏĭls**
ŭll‿ŭlls	**āil‿āils**	**ûrl‿ûrls**
	ēēl‿ēēls	

Notice the same movements as in 1.

B

I. Sentence Practice.

(a) She calls me.
She calls for them.
She calls him up.
She calls on them very often.
She calls for the book at the libary.
He takes it away.
He takes it back.
He takes it up.
He takes it off.
He takes it out of the room.
He takes it with him.
He takes it in fun.
He takes it as a joke.
It looks too hard.
It looks too long.
It looks too easy.
It looks well.
It looks as though it would rain.
She finds there is no way.
She finds there is no time.
She finds there is no use.
She finds there is none left.
She likes to play.
She likes to go to town.

She likes to read aloud.

(b) He walks very fast.
She knocks at my door every morning.
What makes you so cross?
That makes no difference to me.
I shall be sorry if he fails.
What ails you?
Who likes to play bridge?
Who found the balls?
Who saw the fox?
Who broke my box?
Who paid the tax?
Who paid the bills?
Do you think the man paid the bills?
Do you think the boy broke my box?
Which box did he break?
What was in the box?
The box was filled with blocks.
It was the box that was filled with shells.
How many blocks are there in that box?
Will you wind the clocks?
I can see three clocks from my window.
Have you ever been to the Great Lakes?
I wish you would send me some new books.
It takes me too long to do that.
If she takes the five o'clock train, I will meet her at the station.
In case she calls for me, tell her that I will be at home this afternoon.
In case it rains, I shall not go.

(c) Please give me some wax.
How much wax did you buy?
Put the wax in that box.
Do you know where I can find a letter-box?
There is a letter-box in front of our house.
Don't forget to put the letter into the box.
There are many high rocks along the shore.
Let us climb the rocks.

Have you ever seen a fox?
My muff is made of fox fur.
The phlox is a beautiful flower.
He sent her a box of candy.
The box locks.
I cannot find the key to my box.
I sent her a box of books.
What are the names of the books?
I wish you would send me some good books.
What kind of books do you like to read?
I prefer the old books.
I heard the bells ring.
Who rang the bells?
Have you paid your tax-bill?

(d) Have you been to the Falls?
Will you buy me a dozen fresh eggs?
How much are eggs worth now?
Eggs are very high just now.
They expect to return in about three weeks.
We gave them some silver forks for a gift.
Have you seen my new book-racks?
I carved these book-racks.
The trunks have been sent to the station.
The halls were draped with flags.
How many stars are there in our flag?
Where are the Great Lakes?
We are going to spend a few weeks there.
He was here a few weeks ago.
I read those books several years ago.
My brother calls for the books on his way to the library.
He takes them back when he goes to town.
There are some fine oaks in our parks.
We have a number of fine parks.
If he sails on the 15th day of September, he will surely be here by the 1st of October.
If she brings her books, we can study our lesson together.
It takes time to do things well.

II. Vocabulary.

Use these words to form new sentences:

Nouns — rakes, lakes, rocks, flakes, flocks, cakes, rails, halls, balls, bills, pills, tools, shells, clocks, barks, axe, flax, box, phlox, ox, fox.

Verbs — likes, talks, fills, calls, sails, mails, takes, looks, fails, seals, boils, soils, curls.

C — Exercise Story

Did you receive a letter this morning?
Did you receive a letter from your friend?
From whom did you receive a letter?
From whom did you receive a message?
From whom did you receive a present?
Did you receive a present (message) from your friend?
How was the present (message) sent?
The present was sent by a messenger.
The messenger brought the present to me.
The messenger brought the present to me from my friend.
My friend sent a message to me this morning.
Who was the messenger?
The messenger was a boy.
The messenger boy came to my house.
The messenger boy came to my house early this morning.
Early this morning the bell rang and a messenger boy brought me a present.
I received a telephone message this morning.
How much do you have to pay for a telephone message?
How much did you give the messenger boy who brought the message?
Did you give him anything for his trouble?
I will tell you a story about a messenger boy.
Would you like to hear the story?
Have you ever heard the story?
The story is about Dean Swift.

The story is about Dean Swift and the messenger boy.

Who was Dean Swift?

Can you tell me anything about him?

He had a great many friends.

His friends were very kind to him.

His friends often sent him presents.

They were in the habit of sending him presents.

One of his friends often sent him presents.

He always sent them by the same boy.

The boy often came to the Dean's house.

The Dean had never given the boy anything for his trouble.

A friend of Dean Swift's was in the habit of sending him presents which were generally brought by the same servant boy.

Dean Swift had always omitted to give the boy anything for his trouble.

One day the boy came again.

One day the boy called again with a present from his master.

He rang the bell.

He rang the bell and was let into the house.

He was familiar with the house.

He knew where to find the Dean.

He knew where the Dean's room was.

As he knew where to find the Dean, he immediately went up to his room.

He walked up to the door of the study.

He was in a hurry.

He was in such a hurry....

He was in such a hurry that he forgot to knock at the door.

Being in a great hurry that morning, he did not stop to knock at the door.

Without knocking at the door, he pushed it open.

He pushed open the door quickly without knocking.

As soon as he had opened the door he called out, "My master has sent you a present."

One day the messenger came again with a present for the Dean. He rang the bell and was let into the house. Being familiar with the house he knew where to find the Dean and hurried to his study. He pushed open the door and called out, "Here is a present from my master."

The Dean was writing at his table.
The Dean who was writing at his table looked up.
He said, "My boy, that is not the way to deliver a present."
"I will show you how to deliver a present."
"You sit down in my chair."
"You must learn to be more polite."
"I will teach you how to be more polite."
The boy sat down.
The boy sat down in the Dean's chair.
The boy sat down in the Dean's chair at his desk.
The Dean went out of the room.
The Dean left the study.
The Dean left the boy sitting in his chair at the desk.
Presently he knocked at the door.
Presently the boy heard a knock at the door.
When the boy heard a knock at the door, he called, "Come in."
The Dean entered.
The Dean entered the study.
When the Dean entered the study, he said: —
When the Dean entered the study, he said, "If you please, sir."
"If you please, sir," said the Dean, "my master presents his compliments."
"My master presents his compliments and begs that you will accept this present."

The Dean went out of the room, and left the boy sitting in a chair at his desk. Presently the boy heard a knock at the door and when he called, "Come in," the Dean entered the room and said, "If you please, sir, my master presents his compliments and begs that you accept this present."

The boy replied....
The boy replied, "Is that so?"
The boy replied, "Is that so? Return my best thanks to your master."
"Thank your master for me and here is half a crown for you, my boy."
The Dean burst out laughing.
The Dean was much amused.
The Dean was much amused at the boy's reply.

He was so pleased with the boy's remark that he gave him the half crown.

After that....

From that time on....

From that time on whenever the boy came to the Dean's house with a message he was always careful to be polite.

He had learned his lesson well.

DEAN SWIFT AND THE BOY

One day a friend of Dean Swift sent him a present by a servant who had frequently been sent on similar errands, but who had never received the most trifling mark of the Dean's generosity.

Having gained admission, he opened the door of the study, abruptly put down the present and cried very rudely, "Master has sent you a present."

"Young man," said the Dean, rising from his chair, "is that the way you deliver your message? Let me teach you better manners. Sit down in my chair, and I will show you how to behave in future."

The boy sat down and the Dean, going to the door, came up to the table, with a respectful pace, and making a low bow said, "Sir, my master presents his kind compliments, hopes that you are well, and requests your acceptance of a small present."

"Does he?" replied the boy. "Return my best thanks to him, and there is half a crown for you, my boy."

The Dean, thus drawn into an act of generosity, laughed heartily and gave the boy a crown for his wit.

LESSON XX

A

I. d and **t** before a vowel.

These belong to consonants of Class **II** and are explosive sounds.

For **d** and **t** the tip of the tongue is placed behind the upper gum and the sides touch the upper side teeth. The breath is forced out between the teeth and the tongue falls back into its flat position. It is this movement that we see in the lower jaw which is the visible characteristic. We have the same movement for **k,** hard **c** and **g,** but in **d** and **t** it is somewhat plainer.

Note. In practicing syllables in this lesson take only **d.**

II. Mirror Practice on Sounds.

1. Compare: —

ä‿**d**ä	ē‿**d**ē
ō‿**d**ō	ī‿**d**ī
ōō‿**d**ōō	öû‿**d**öû
ā‿**d**ā	ür‿**d**ür
	âw‿**d**âw

Notice the jaw movement in syllables beginning with **d.**

2. Syllable drill leading up to a sentence.

dē	**fi**	
dē	**si**	
dē	**pri**	
dē	**fē**	
dē	**sē**	
mā	**dē**	**sē**
mā	**rē**	**sē**
mā	**rē**	**si**
mā	**dē**	**si**

She may decide to do so.

d and **t** are practiced more in sentences than in syllables.

B

I. Sentence Practice.

(a) What did you do?
How did you do it?
Why did you do it?
Did you do it?
Did you see it?
I did not see it.
I did not see you do it.
I did not think that you would do it.
Why do you do it now?
Do you think she will do it?
Do you think he did it?
Why do you think he did it?
Did they do it?
Don't do it.
Don't do that now.
Did you say that?
Will you do it soon?
Did you know that I did it?
Do you know how to do it?
Do you know how they did it?

Do you know why he did it?
Do you think that you can do it?
Don't think of doing it.
I did not dare to do it.
Do you feel sure of it?
Do you feel sure that we ought to do it?
I think it ought to be done.
How much did you do?
How much have you done?
I doubt whether I can do it.
I doubt whether I can do it today.
I doubt whether that is the right way to do it.
I doubt whether it can be done in that way.
I didn't know that it would be done so well.
Don't you think that it will be done on time?
Don't you know how to do it?
Didn't you know the way?
Didn't they show you how to do it?
Does he do the work well?
Does he know how it should be done?
Do it or not, just as you please.
I do think he ought to do better, don't you?
Do you know how much there is to be done?

(b) Do you know how to play that game?
Do you think it will do?
Do you care to go to the dance?
Do it now.
Do it again.
Do it later.
Do it over again.
Do to others as you would that they should do to you.
It is time to go.
It is time to do it.
It is time to see it.
It is time to think it over.
It is time to send it off.
It is too far.
It is too hard.
It is too late.

It is too much.
It is too long.
It is too dark.
It is too deep.
Tell me about the dance.
Tell them what to do.
Tell the man to take it away.
Tell him how you wish to have it done.
Tell them to take it off.

(c) What daily paper do you read?
She told me that she would come daily.
I wish you would teach me how to do it.
I taught her daughter how to do it.
Do not talk so loud. You will disturb them.
Do not let that disturb you.
The door was opened by the maid.
Who told you that?
He told us that there was no danger.
I doubt if they will tell us about their plan today.
There is no doubt about it.
On what date did they arrive?
They were to arrive yesterday, but the fog was so dense that the ship could not dock in time.
What time will they reach the dock?
I doubt if they will dock today.
It would doubtless be well to do that right away.
The waves dashed over the deck of the ship.
It is so damp that we cannot go out on deck.
Shall we have some tea?
This tea tasted very good.
How does your tea taste?
Have you ever read "Over the Tea-cups?"
This tea came from China.
Will you take tea with me this evening?
My tea is too strong.
I don't care for strong tea.

(d) What time did you arrive on Tuesday?

They arrived on Tuesday, the twenty-first day of December.
What day is today?
I think it is your duty to go today.
What time did you have your dinner?
We had turkey for dinner.
Will you dine with us tomorrow?
What time do you dine?
They will dine with us on Tuesday.
I gave the boy a dime.
A dime is a tenth of a dollar.
Did you have a good time today?
Will you let me see your time-table?
Please get me a time-table when you go to town today.
I am going down-town today to buy a table for the dining-room.
We have a new tea table.
Did you talk to him about it?
Please don't talk to me now.
Don't talk about it.
I'm tired of hearing them talk about it.
Play the tune over.
I taught him to play that tune.
To whom does that dog belong?
Don't tease the dog.
What is your dog's name?
Did you go to the dog-show?
The team stopped in front of the door.
Today is the tenth of December.
Come and dine with us the day after tomorrow.
We have dinner at six o'clock.

II. Vocabulary.

Use these words to form new sentences:

NOUNS — dome, dough, dew, daisy, dainty, dame, date, daughter, day, dawn, deed, dean, deer, dime, dog, dove, doubt, time, tie, tide, tire, tooth, tool, top, tower, town, toy, toast, toad.

VERBS — darn, do, dance, dare, dash, dip, toil, tip, tie, time.

ADJECTIVES OR ADVERBS — dark, damp, dear, deep, down, tired, together, today, too.

C — Exercise Story

Have you ever been abroad?
Have you ever been in Paris?
Did you visit the French Academy?
Did you go to a meeting of the French Academy?
Do you speak French?
Do you understand French well enough to attend a meeting?
Is the meeting public?
Is it a public meeting?
Is it open to the public?
Where do you get cards for admission?
Where do you get tickets?
How much are they?
What is the price of admission?
Perhaps I can get permission to go to the meeting.
Several years ago....
Some time ago....
A great many years ago....
A great many years ago Benjamin Franklin was abroad.
When Franklin was abroad....
When Franklin was in Paris....
When Franklin was in Paris he attended a meeting.
He attended a public meeting of the French Academy.
He did not understand French well.
He did not speak the language fluently.
He spoke but little French.
But he wished to be polite.
But he wished to be polite and applaud at the right time.
He did not understand French well enough to be able to follow all that was said.
What did he do?
What did he decide to do?

He decided to watch one of his friends.

He decided to watch a lady that he knew.

One of his acquaintances was there.

One of his acquaintances was at the meeting.

One of his acquaintances was at the meeting and he decided to watch her.

He decided that he would applaud whenever she did so.

Franklin decided to watch one of his acquaintances in the audience and applaud whenever she did so.

After the meeting....

After the meeting his little grandson said to him....

He said to him, "Why did you applaud only when they praised you?"

"Did you know that you applauded only when they praised you?"

Franklin was obliged to admit....

Franklin was obliged to admit that he did not understand much French.

Franklin was obliged to admit that he did not understand French and therefore had applauded only when his friend had done so.

BENJAMIN FRANKLIN

One day while Benjamin Franklin was in Paris he attended a meeting at the French Academy.

He did not understand much French, but he wished to be polite and applaud at the right moment.

Therefore, he decided to watch one of his friends in the audience and applaud whenever she did so.

After the meeting his little grandson said to him, "Why did you applaud louder than anyone else when your name was mentioned?"

Franklin was obliged to admit that he did not understand French and therefore had applauded only when his friend did so.

LESSON XXI

A

I. dr and **tr** before a vowel.

dr and **tr** have the same forward movement as in the combinations in Lessons **VIII** and **IX.**

As they look alike, we practice only one of these in syllables.

II. Mirror Practice on Sounds.

1. Difference between: —

dä‿**drä**	dē‿**drē**
dō‿**drō**	dī‿**drī**
dōō‿**drōō**	döû‿**dröû**
dā‿**drā**	dâ‿**drâ**

Notice the forward movement in the syllables containing the **r.**

2. Pronounce rapidly: —

the day — the **dr**ay
the tea — the **tr**ee
the doubt — the **tr**out
the dive — the **dr**ive
the team — the **dr**eam

In the above exercise, do not try to distinguish between **d** and **t,** — merely note the forward movement in the words containing the **r** before the vowel.

Be sure to speak naturally, repeating the words often.

B

I. Sentence Practice.

(a) Try again.
Try to do it today.
Try to do it soon.
Try not to think about it.
Try to remember.
Try to forget it.
Try once more.
Try to do something.
Try not to notice it.
Try to do it now before it is too late.
"If at first you don't succeed, try, try again."
Is it true that he missed the train?
Is it true that they have given up their trip?
I shall try to come early, but do not wait for me.
He will try hard for the prize.
Try to send it to me by Saturday.
You ought to try for her sake.
I tried to recall the story that you told me the other day, but I could not remember it.
If he tries I think he will succeed.
I trust that you will try to do your best.
We trust that you will come.
We trust you absolutely.
You must trust to your own judgment.
It was a very trying time for us all.
Did you try for the first prize?

(b) Did they drive away?
Did they drive up to the house?
When did they drive to the park?
What time did they say they would drive over?
Do you like to drive through the woods?
Tell the conductor to give you a transfer.
You must transfer at the subway.
Where is the transfer station?
Do you like to travel by rail?

He travels a great deal.
The driver told us that it was a long drive.
The drive through the woods was very pleasant.
The boys have had a drill.
What time did the drill begin?
The drill began at three.
The troops were drilling.
Can you draw?
I wish you would try to draw the picture for me.
Let us draw lots.
The boys drew lots to see which one should go.
The flowers are beginning to droop.
They have not had a drop of water.
Is that a true story?
Do you think that dreams ever come true?
What did you dream?
I had a dreadful dream last night.

(c) They have been away on a short trip.
How did you enjoy your trip through the mountains?
The boy taught his dog a number of tricks.
They played a trick on him.
What train shall we take?
Come on the early train.
That is an express train.
This train does not stop at our station.
The train was late.
Our train was half an hour late this morning.
I have bought a Japanese tray.
What kind of a tree is that?
There are some beautiful trees along our driveway.
The children are to have a Christmas-tree.
Will you help me trim the tree?
What's the trouble?
How long will it take you to pack your trunk?
The expressman put the trunk on the truck.
Did the boy tell the truth about the matter?
He has never told me an untruth.
A man was drowned in the river the other day.
That's not true.

He drew the picture very well.
My brother drew the first prize in drawing.
They have a beautiful drawing-room in their new house.
Put the paper in the upper drawer of my desk.
You will find it in the right-hand drawer.

(d) There is a bench under the tree.
Put the cups on the tray.
It was very careless of you to drop the glass.
It was kind of you to draw the picture for me.
It would be well for him to try for the prize.
It is almost a mile to the nearest drug-store.
It is too early for the train.
What time did the trial begin?
The man was put on trial.
The trial began at ten o'clock.
We are having very dry weather.
The season has been very dry.
We drove to the drug-store for the medicine.
We could not get the medicine at the village drug-store.
We met the tramp on the road.
A tramp came to our house this morning.
We saw the troops pass by.
A troop of soldiers passed by our house.
Did you hear the drum?
The boy beat the drum.
They have been trying to sell their house for the last two years.
We tried in vain to persuade them to go.
Can we trust you not to betray us?
The boy blew his trumpet.
I bought a toy trumpet for the boy.

II. Vocabulary.

These words may be used to form new sentences:

NOUNS — dream, drama, drop, dress, draught, truth, tree, Troy, train, trail, dray, trade, troop, trip, trial, trouble.

VERBS — try, drive, drove, draw, drew, drop, drown, drink, drank, drift, dread, drape, drill, trill.

ADJECTIVES — dreary, dreadful.

C — Exercise Story

Do you like to walk?
Do you like to walk in the country?
Do you like to walk early in the morning?
Walking is a healthful exercise.
Walking in the country is a healthful exercise.
I like to go to walk with my friend.
My friend asked me to go to walk with him.
One day a friend of Mark Twain asked him to go to walk.
One morning Mark Twain was busy writing at his desk, when a friend came in.
He asked him to go to walk.
He asked the author to go to walk.
The author said to his friend, "Where are you going?"
"I have an errand to do," replied the friend.
Do you ever have errands to do?
Do you like to do errands?
Do you like to go out into the country?
Mark Twain's friend had an errand to do in the country.
Was it far?
Do you like to walk far?
"How far is it?" asked Mark Twain.
The friend replied, "Oh, about a mile."
Have you ever walked a mile?
How long does it take to walk a mile?
Mark Twain's friend wanted him to walk a mile with him.
Was the author willing to go?
Did he want to go?
Of course he was glad to go.
"Of course I'll go," said Mark Twain.
"Of course I'll go if I must."

"Of course I'll go," said Mark Twain, "because the Bible says I must."

What does the Bible say?

What does the Bible have to do with it?

"The Bible!" exclaimed the friend.

"What in the world has the Bible to do with it?"

Mark Twain replied, "It distinctly says, 'If a man ask thee to walk with him a mile, go with him twain.' "

MARK TWAIN'S WIT

One morning Mark Twain was busy writing at his desk when a friend came in and asked him to go to walk.

"Where are you going?" asked the author.

"Out into the country. I have an errand to do," said the friend.

"How far is it?" asked Mark Twain.

"Oh, about a mile," said the friend.

"Of course, I'll go," said the author, "The Bible says I must."

"The Bible!" exclaimed the friend, "What in the world has the Bible to do with it?"

Mark Twain replied, "It distinctly says, 'If a man ask thee to walk with him a mile, go with him twain.' "

LESSON XXII

A

I. sh, ch, j and soft **g** before a vowel.

These all look alike, as may be illustrated by pronouncing the following words: —

Ger-man
Sher-man
Jer-sey
Cher-burg

or

the **sh**op — the **ch**op
the **ch**est — the **j**est

Having practiced the **sh** in the first lesson, there is no further syllable drill to practice before the mirror in this lesson.

B

I. Sentence Practice.

(a) Can you change this bill for me?
Count your change before you leave.
We change cars at the subway.
Let us change our subject.
If you change your mind, let me know.
Have they changed the time?
Why did you change the time?
What changes have been made in the plans?
I think they will change it for you if you wish.
Will you change places with me?
How much did they charge you for it?

Charge it to me.
It will be charged to him.
Shall I have it charged, or shall I pay for it?
How much does he charge by the hour?
He will take charge of the work.
I think they have over-charged you.
I will give you one more chance.
That will be your last chance to go.
There is not much chance of that.
Give him another chance.
That will be a good chance to see them.
You must take your chances.
I met him by chance.
By chance I met them on the street this morning.

(b) That will do just as well.
That will be just the thing.
That will be just as far.
We were just in time.
You may do just as you please.
Just as you say.
Just think a moment.
Just think it over.
That is just the trouble.
That is just what I want.
That is just what I think.
That will do just as well I am sure.
I think it is just the same size.
Go just as far as you can.
Come just as often as you can.
Do just as you please about it.
Do just as you think best.
He can do that just as well as not.
I might just as well do it now and be done with it.
Just as soon as I hear from them I will let you know.
I am ready to do just as you think best.
Just now I have nothing more for you to do.
Just at present I do not wish for any more.
They have just come home from a long journey.
We reached the station just as the train came in.

(c) Show me the check.
Show me the chain.
Show me the chart.
Show me the gem.
Show me the jar.
Show me the cheese.
Show me the way to church.
Are you going to church?
To which church do you belong?
The chapel is not far from the church.
We can see the church spire from our window.
I heard the chimes.
The chimes were ringing just as we passed the church.
Give me the check.
I sent him a check.
Where can I have this check cashed?
Do you believe they will cash the check for me at the bank?
Will you have the baggage checked?
Be careful not to lose your check.
Give him the check for your trunk.
We must start early because we must have our baggage checked.
Have you ever studied German?
You will have a chance to speak German with them.
Have you read the first chapter of the new book?
I have just finished the third chapter.
How many chapters are there?
Do not read more than one chapter.
I bought a jar of cream.
They charged me fifteen cents for a jar of cream.
Did you buy some cheese?
This cheese is very good.
I am fond of cream cheese.
They have very good cream cheese in that shop.

(d) May I have my choice?
Choose whichever one you please.
You have made a wise choice.
He chose to remain at home.
Which one did you choose?

How did you enjoy your journey to Japan?
They are going to Japan in June.
Have you ever been to China?
My friend will remain in China a few weeks.
He has been on a long journey.
He has just come home from a journey around the world.
We shall start on our journey in June.
They arrived on the first of June.
Where shall you spend the 4th of July?
Last Fourth of July we were on board the ship.
They came home in January.
I think they will enjoy their journey.
I should enjoy going with them.
How did you enjoy your journey?
I should prefer to go to Japan.
You must be sure to go if you have a chance.
It would be a good chance for them to go.

II. Vocabulary.

Use these words to form new sentences:

Nouns — chart, choice, chance, chain, change, cheese, charm, cheek, chin, church, chimes, chapel, chance, check, chalk, charge, cheer, chief, child, jay, joy, jest, jewel, James, gem, German, germ, Japan, China, jar, June, jury.

Verbs — change, choose, charge, chop, cheer, chase, charm, jar, join, joke, judge, chirp, chew.

Adjectives — Japanese, Chinese, just, cheap.

C — Exercise Story

Once upon a time...
Not very long ago...
Not very long ago there was an old farmer.
He lived on his farm.

He lived in the country.

He had always lived in the country.

Do you prefer to live in the country or in the city?

Have you ever been in the country?

Have you ever been to school in the country?

Have you ever been to a country school.

The farmer had never been to school.

The farmer had not had the opportunity of attending school.

When he was a boy he had not had the opportunity of attending school.

Consequently he was not a scholar.

When he grew old...

As he grew old...

In his old age...

In his old age he could not read at all.

At the present time...

Nowadays...

Nowadays children always go to school.

Nowadays our children always go to school.

Nowadays our children have the opportunity of attending school.

There was another old man.

The farmer knew another old man.

The farmer knew another gray-headed old man.

The other man was his neighbor.

He saw his neighbor one day.

One day he saw his neighbor.

One day he saw his neighbor sitting at the window.

One day he saw his neighbor sitting at the window reading.

One day he saw his neighbor sitting at the window with spectacles on his nose, reading the paper.

He had never before seen this man with spectacles.

He had never before seen this man reading.

He had never seen such a sight.

Never before had he seen such a sight.

The sight aroused him.

The sight aroused his curiosity.

The sight made him wish...

The sight made him wish to be able to read.

The sight made him wish to be able to read the paper, too.

Do you read the newspaper?

Are you fond of reading?

Do you like to read?

The old farmer made up his mind...

The old farmer decided...

The old farmer decided that he would buy a pair of spectacles.

The old farmer decided that he would purchase a pair of spectacles.

The old farmer decided that he would purchase a pair of spectacles at the first opportunity.

Soon after this...

Some time after...

Some time after this he was obliged to go to the city.

Some time after this he was obliged to go to the city with a load of wood.

Not long after this he had to take a load of wood to town.

Soon after this, he made a journey to the city to sell a load of wood.

After he had sold the wood...

After the wood was sold...

After the wood was sold he thought of the spectacles.

He asked someone...

He asked a young man...

He asked a young man where he could buy them.

"Will you please show me where to buy spectacles?" he said to a young man who passed by.

This young man showed him a shop.

This young man showed him the shop of an optician.

This young man directed him to the shop of an optician.

The old man went into the shop.

The old man entered the shop.

The old man entered the shop and spoke to the optician.

He told the optician what he wanted.

The optician looked at the farmer's eyes.

He examined the farmer's eyes.

He tested the farmer's eyes.

He made a thorough test of the farmer's eyes.

He used the proper means to test the farmer's eyes.
He tried one pair of spectacles after another.
He made one trial after another.
He tried all the spectacles he had.
He tried almost his whole stock of spectacles.
But it was of no use.
But it was in vain.
But in vain, none of them would fit.
But in vain, no pair would fit.
Finally the optician believed...
Finally the optician began to believe...
Finally the optician began to believe that something was wrong.
Something must be wrong.
Something must be the matter.
Something must be amiss.
"My good man," said the optician.
"My good fellow," said the optician.
"My good fellow, do you know how to read?"
"Can you read?"
"Can I read?"
"Do I know how to read?"
"Do I know how to read?" was the reply.
"Of course not."
"Of course I cannot read."
"If I could read would I be here?"
"If I could read would I come to you?"
"If I could read would I come to you to pay you money for spectacles?"

THE FARMER AND THE SPECTACLES

There was once an old farmer, who as a boy, had not had the opportunity of attending school as our children have nowadays. Consequently, he was not a very great scholar when he was a boy, and in his later years could not read at all. He had a neighbor, also a gray-headed man.

One day he saw this neighbor sitting at the window, with spectacles on his nose, reading the paper. He had never before seen this man with spectacles, and had never seen him reading. This sight aroused the desire in him to be able to read the paper, too. He made up his mind that he would buy a pair of spectacles at the first opportunity.

Soon after this he had to take a load of wood to the city. After the wood was sold, he thought of the spectacles. He asked a young man where he could buy that article. This young man showed him the shop of an optician. The old man entered and made his want known. The optician was ready to make a sale, and he used the proper means to test the farmer's eyes. He made one trial after another, and tried almost his whole stock of spectacles; but in vain; no pair would suit.

The optician finally believed that something was wrong, and said, "My good man, can you read?"

"Can I read?" was the reply. "Of course I cannot read. If I could, would I come to you to pay you money for spectacles?"

LESSON XXIII

A

I. sp (or **sm**), **spr**, **st** (or **sn**), **str** (or **scr**)*, **sw**, and **sl.**

Note. In this lesson, we have no new letter, the above being common combinations, however, should be practiced.

For the mirror practice, two of these combinations will be given at a time and they are to be practiced in order. Some of them look so nearly alike that it is not wise to attempt to see any difference. They will rarely be confused in sentences if the vowel is correctly seen.

II. Mirror Practice on Sounds.

1. Difference between: —

spä‿sprä
spō‿sprō
spōō‿sprōō
spā‿sprā
spē‿sprē
spī‿sprī
spöû‿spröû
spâ‿sprâ

Notice that in the above group, the syllables containing **r** show a forward movement before the vowel, and that they are longer.

*str and scr, although not formed alike are, in outward appearance, almost identical.

2. Difference between: —

stä‿strä
stō‿strō
stōō‿strōō
stā‿strā
stē‿strē
stī‿strī
stöû‿ströû
stâ‿strâ

See note under **1.**

3. Difference between: —

snō‿slō
snōō‿slōō
snā‿slā
snē‿slē
snī‿slī
snöû‿slöû

Note. **sl** before a vowel has already been practiced in Lesson **X** (see note).

In **sn** the tongue movement is not plain and the words in this group must be read by the context.

4. Difference between: —

sō‿**swō**
sōō‿**swōō**
sā‿**swā**
sē‿**swē**
sī‿**swī**
sâ‿**swâ**

Note. In words containing **w** there is a decided forward movement in both lips before the vowel.

B

I. Sentence Practice.

(a) Speak to him.
Speak slowly.
Do not speak about it.
I would not speak about it.
If I were in your place I should speak to him about it.
You must speak slowly.
You ought to have spoken about it before this.
Speak louder.
Speak up for it.
Speak slowly.
Speak distinctly.
Stand up.
Stand straight.
Do not stand on the sidewalk.
How did your father stand the journey?
He stood it very well.
Stand still a moment.
It stands to reason that he will go.
Shall you stay there very long?
They must not stay up too late.
Stay here.
Stay with us over night.
It must stay where it belongs.
Don't stay away too long.
She is still thinking about it.
He is still at work.
They will stay with us until next Spring.
What time did you start?
Shall you start tomorrow?
Can you stop there on your way to the station?

(b) Will you spend the day with me?
How much money did you spend?
I spent all I had.
I have spent a great deal of time over it.

Don't spend too much time on it.
Can you spare the time now?
I can spare a few of them if you want some.
Have you a stamp to spare?
I have none to spare.
Stop the car.
Stop there for the present.
Please step to one side.
Step back.
I bought some stamps at the post-office.
Put a special delivery stamp on your letter.
I will stop at the news-stand and buy a paper.
Everything was at a stand-still.
There is a news-stand at the station.
There is a new store on State Street.
Have you seen our State House?
We can see the dome of the State House from our window.
There is a statue in front of the State House.
How many States are there in the Union?
Can you name the Southern States?
Did you have a good state-room on board the ship?
The state-rooms on the new ships are fine.

(c) I am going to Spain next spring.
I am studying Spanish this winter.
I shall spend some time there.
Last year we went to Switzerland.
We traveled all over Switzerland.
Have you ever been to Scotland?
We spent the summer in the Scottish Highlands.
Have you ever read Scott's "Lady of the Lake"?
The Scotch people are noted for their thrift.
Are you fond of Sir Walter Scott's novels?
How do you spell that word?
The spell was broken.
This flower smells sweet.
Do you think it will storm today?
I am afraid they will have to stay at home if it storms.
How it stormed yesterday!

I hope the storm will be over before they start.
Tell the maid to sweep the stairs.
The boys strove to win the game.
The man was required to sweep the side-walk in front of the store every morning.
Come up-stairs with me.
The stream has swept away the bridge.
Where is the screw-driver?
Will you go for a stroll with me?
How far is it from the station to the store?
It is only a few steps.
Did you ever try to walk on skiis?

(d) The man made a long speech.
That was a strange story that he told us.
There was a stowaway in the steamer.
It is strange that we have not heard from them.
I have planted some sweet-peas in my garden.
Have you any string beans in your garden?
We can see the ship with the spy-glass.
That is a beautiful spray of apple blossoms.
The men must spray the trees.
I have sprained my wrist.
That is a bad sprain.
I found this scrap of paper on the street.
The church stands on the corner of the street.
We can see the church spire from our window.
The church has a high steeple.
There is a clock on the church spire.
He did that on the spur of the moment.
Give me a spool of black thread.
The spoon is made of silver.
She gave me a scarf for a Christmas present.
The man has a scar on his face.
Can you describe the stranger who came to the door?
Can you sketch?
Let me see your sketch-book?
Have you read Irving's "Sketch-book"?
How far is the skating rink from our school?

II. Vocabulary.

Use these words to form new sentences:

NOUNS — spark, sparrow, spoke, spell, spire, spy, spoon, spool, stove, steam, straw, stream, street, stroll, spray, smoke, scroll, scrawl, screen, scribe, slope, snake, snow, Spanish, spruce, swan, screw.

VERBS — spell, sprout, stoop, stay, stray, strike, strew, spray, sway, spoke, scream, sleep, sneeze, stir.

ADJECTIVES — spry, steep, stern, sly, Spanish, spare, small, smooth.

C — Exercise Story

Where is the servant?
Has the servant gone out?
Has the servant gone out on an errand?
Who sent the servant on an errand?
Do you like to do errands?
Will you do an errand for me?
I did several errands this morning.
One day . . . .
One day a gentleman sent his servant on an errand.
He sent his servant on an errand to the Governor's house.
A gentleman sent his servant to the Governor's office.
One day a gentleman sent his servant to the Governor's office with a letter.
The servant delivered the letter.
The servant returned home.
The servant returned from his errand.
Soon after the servant returned home.
When the servant returned home . . .
When he returned home the gentleman said to him, "John, did you give the Governor my letter?"
"Yes, sir," replied the boy.
"Yes, sir, I gave the note to the Governor."
Can he read the letter?

Can you read the letter?

Could you read the letter?

Could the Governor read the letter?

If the Governor cannot read....

If the Governor cannot read the letter there is not use writing to him.

The servant said, "Yes, sir, I gave the letter to the Governor, but there's no use writing letters to him, he can't read."

The gentleman did not know that the Governor could not read.

He was surprised that the Governor could not read.

Why couldn't he read?

Was the letter written in English?

Was it written in Spanish?

Was it written in German?

Was it written in Italian?

Could you read the letter if it were written in Italian?

The Governor could not read the letter because he was blind.

The servant said, "The Governor is blind."

"He is blind as a bat."

The servant told his master that he had given the Governor the letter. "But," said the boy, "there's no use writing letters to him; he can't read. He's blind as a bat."

The gentleman did not believe that the Governor was blind.

"Is he blind?" he asked.

"Blind!" he exclaimed.

"Yes, sir," replied the boy, "he's blind."

How did the servant know that he was blind?

Did the Governor speak to the boy?

The gentleman exclaimed, "Blind! Is he blind?"

"Yes, sir; blind. Twice he asked me where my hat was and I had it on my head all the time. Blind as a bat, sir!"

BLIND AS A BAT

One day a gentleman sent his servant to the Governor with a letter. When the servant returned from his errand the gentleman said to him, "Well, John, did you give the Governor my note?"

"Yes, sir; I gave it to him; but there's no use writing him letters; he can't read them. He's blind — blind as a bat!"

"Blind!"

"Yes, sir; blind. Twice he asked me where my hat was, and I had it on my head all the time. Blind as a bat, sir!"

LESSON XXIV

A

I. q.

This letter is a combination of **k** and **wh** (**k‿wh**).

II. Mirror Practice on Sounds.

1. Difference between: —

cŏ‿quŏ
că‿quă
kĕ‿quĕ
kĭ‿quĭ
câ‿quâ

Notice that in syllables beginning with hard **c** or **k** we see only a cheek and jaw movement, while in **q** we have the cheek and jaw movement followed by a forward movement before the vowel.

2. Difference between: —

quĕ‿squĕ
quĭ‿squĭ
quâ‿squâ

Notice in **quē, quī** and **quâ** the mouth remains open, while in **squē, squī** and **squâ** the mouth is closed at the beginning of the syllable by bringing the teeth apparently together.

B

I. Sentence Practice.

(a) Be quick about it.
Do your work quickly.
She was very quick about it.
How quickly the time flies!
Do it as quickly as you can.
Come back as quickly as possible.
Can you quote the remark?
I am not quite sure.
It is quite remarkable how much they have accomplished.
You are quite right.
It is quite likely that they will go.
The man is quite reliable.
It is quite possible that they have heard about it.
I think it is quite probable.
That is not quite enough.
It is not quite fine enough.
This one is not quite so long as the other one.
The thread is not quite coarse enough.
This one is quite as good.
You are quite right, we should have more.

(b) What was the question?
Did you answer all the questions?
How many questions did they ask?
There is no question about it, she is right.
It was out of the question that he should fail.
Unquestionably that would be the best way.
It will require more time.
Much will be required of them.
It requires more than I thought.
Will you inquire about the train?
Have you made any inquiries?
Please inquire about it.
It is quite possible that we shall go.

The child is very quiet.
Keep quiet about it.
How quiet it seems here.
He must be more quiet about his work.
What a queer question to ask us!
He asks such queer questions.
That was a queer mistake.

(c) Please buy a quart of milk.
Milk is sold at nine cents a quart.
How many quarts are there in a gallon?
That is not the right quantity.
That is poor quality.
You must buy a better quality.
The cloth must be of a fine quality.
It is the quality not the quantity that counts.
Have you ever been to Quebec?
Quebec is a quaint old town.
Please repeat the question.
I prefer the square table.
Can you write with a quill pen?
The amethyst is purple quartz.
I have bought a quill for my hat.
Did you hear the quartet play?
They have a beautiful choir in that church.
Go to the drug store and buy some quinine.
Take some quinine for your cold.
Do you like quinze jelly?

(d) They came home at a quarter before two.
Can you lend me a quarter?
I picked a quart of berries.
It was not quite a full quart.
That is not quite so much as I asked for, but it will do.
It is quite impossible for them to come today.
It was not quite a quarter before twelve when they arrived.
Are you quite sure that this is as good as you can make it?
We saw the queen yesterday.

I should like to see the Queen of Holland.
Did you inquire at what time the queen would drive in the park?
Have you ever seen such a quaint old town before?
I am quite sure that they will be here in a quarter of an hour.
Will you buy me a quire of note-paper?
How many sheets are there in a quire?
The quotation seems very familiar.
Can you quote the exact words?
I have a beautiful old quilt that my grandmother made for me.
Did you ever go to a quilting party?
Is he qualified for that position?
Come back in a quarter of an hour.

II. Vocabulary.

Use these words to form new sentences:

NOUNS — quality, quantity, quarrel, quart, quarter, queen, quest, question, quill, quire (choir), quotation, squire, square, Quaker.

VERBS — quote, question, qualify, quarter.

ADJECTIVES — quaint, quick, quite, queer.

C — Exercise Story

This story is about Walter Scott.
Who was Sir Walter Scott?
Can you tell me where he was born?
Where did he live? He lived in Scotland.
He was born in the year 1771.
When he was a boy,....
When he was a boy at the High School,....
When he was a boy at the High School of Edinburg,....

When he was a boy at the High School of Edinburg, he was very studious.

He was a studious boy.

He was a very studious boy.

He was such a studious boy.

He wished to be at the head of the class.

He tried to be at the head of the class.

He tried to get above another boy.

He tried in vain to get above another boy.

He tried in vain to get above another boy who was always at the head.

When Sir Walter Scott was a boy at the High School of Edinburg, he tried in vain to get above another boy who was always at the head of the class.

He had seen....observed....noticed....

The boy had noticed....

He had noticed....

Sir Walter Scott had noticed....

When Sir Walter Scott had noticed....

As soon as Sir Walter Scott noticed....

Before long Sir Walter Scott noticed why the other boy was always at the head.

I will ask you a question.

They asked me a question.

They were asked a question.

The boys were asked a question.

When the boys were asked a question....

The boys were asked a question at school.

One morning, when the boys were asked a question at school....

The boy played.

The boy played in school.

The boy played in school with a button on his waistcoat.

The boy at the head of the class played with the button on his waistcoat.

One morning, when the boys were asked a question, Walter Scott noticed that when the boy at the head of the class was addressed he always played with a button on his waistcoat.

Will you help me?

Will you please help me?

It may help him.
It seemed to help him.
That always seemed to help him.
The boy answered the questions.
The boy gave the answers.
The boy gave the right answer.
The boy gave the correct answer.
He always gave the correct answer.
He invariably gave the correct answer.
He invariably gave the correct answer to all the questions.
The answer was correct.
Do you think he will give the correct answer?
Do you think he can answer the questions correctly?
I am sure he will fail.
He will fail to answer the questions.
Do not fail to answer the questions.
The question was asked.
The question was asked by the teacher.
It was out of the question.
It was out of the question that he would fail.

You may depend upon it, he will not fail to answer the question correctly.

He will take pains to answer all the questions correctly.

When the boys in Walter Scott's school (class) were asked a question, the boy at the head of the class always played with a particular button on his waistcoat. That seemed to help him, for he invariably answered all the questions correctly.

What will you do about it?
What did you do about it?
What did he do about it?
What did the boy do about it?
What did Scott do?
What did Scott manage to do?
What did Scott manage to get away from the boy?
He knew how.
He knew how to cut off the button.
The boy knew.
The boy knew about it.
The boy knew nothing about it.

It is certain that the boy knew nothing about it.

He was not aware of it.

He did not become aware of it.

He did not become aware of the fact that he had lost his button.

One day Walter Scott managed to cut the button off from the waistcoat of the boy without having the latter become aware of his loss.

When the time comes....

When the time came....

When the time came to ask the question....

As soon as it was time to ask the question....

Question time came.

Question time came and the boy at the head of the class was asked a question.

He missed the button.

Now he missed the button.

It was not until then that he missed the button.

He missed the familiar button.

He could not find it.

He was perplexed.

He was disturbed.

He was so disturbed about it.

This disturbed him.

This disturbed his mind so much.

The fact that he had lost his familiar button disturbed his mind so much....

He forgot.

He forgot the answer.

We were much surprised that he had forgotten the answer.

Much to our surprise he forgot to answer the question.

Imagine the surprise of the class when the boy failed to answer the question and Walter Scott took his place.

WALTER SCOTT AT SCHOOL

The following anecdote is found in Scott's autobiography.

"There was," says Walter Scott, "a boy in my class who always stood at the head, and I cound not, with all my efforts, supplant him. Day after day he kept his place. At length I observed that when a question was asked him, he always fumbled with his fingers at a particular button on the lower part of his waistcoat while seeking an answer. I thought, therefore, if I could remove the button slyly, the surprise at not finding it, might derange his ideas at the next interrogation of the class, and give me a chance of taking him down. The button was, therefore, removed without his perceiving it. Great was my anxiety to know the success of my measure, and it succeeded but too well.

"The hour of interrogation arrived, and the boy was questioned. As usual, he sought with his fingers the friendly button, but he could not find it. Disconcerted, he looked down: the talisman was gone, his ideas became confused, he could not reply. I seized the opportunity, answered the question, and took his place, which he never recovered, nor do I believe he ever suspected the author of the trick.

"I have often met him since we entered the world, and never without feeling my conscience reproach me. Frequently have I resolved to make him some amends by rendering him a service; but an opportunity did not present itself, and I fear I did not seek one with as much ardour as I sought to supplant him at school."

LESSON XXV

A

Note. The letter **l** has been practiced in several lessons and should be familiar (see Lessons **X** and **XI**) but no special attention has been given to words beginning with **l** (**l**amp, **l**ip, **l**ook, etc.)

Study **l** before a vowel in sentences under **B.**

B

I. Sentence Practice.

(a) When did they leave?
Did they leave early?
I must leave.
He must have left.
I may leave early.
I shall leave it to him.
Can we leave it to them?
Do you think that we can leave it to her?
Do you think that we can leave tomorrow?
Leave it to me.
Leave it to them by all means.
I should leave it to them by all means.
If I were in your place I should leave tomorrow.
They may leave on the three o'clock train.
He left on that train.
He left early.
They left town last Monday.
He had left when I called.
He had left in a hurry.
He had left it at home.
It was left over.

It was left until the last moment.
It was left here this morning.
It was left by the postman early this morning.
In case he leaves the book with me I will write and let you know.

(b) Let us look it up.
Let us look it over.
Let us look about.
Let us look at it.
Let us look on the bright side.
Let us lose no time.
Let us look at the house.
Let us lend it to him.
Let us light the gas.
Let us lift it up.
Let us lock the door.
Let me have it.
Let me know.
Let me tell you all about it.
Let me show you how.
Let me go with you.
Let me know if it will be convenient for you to go next week.
Let me buy the book for you on my way to town.
Let me hear the story again before you go.
Let me have one more if you please.
Let me tell you the story as it was told to me.
Let me show you how to fold the paper.
Let me show you where they live.
They live in the large house on the left.
How is their new house lighted?
Our house is lighted by electricity.

(c) Did you go to the lecture this afternoon?
What was the subject of his lecture?
Can you follow a lecturer by reading his lips?
His lips were easy to read.
The lecture was very interesting.
The last lecture was too long.

Who is the lecturer to be?
Lay the book on my desk.
Where did they land?
We landed at Liverpool.
We landed at Liverpool late last night.
Did you go to London?
Will you go for a sail with me on the lake?
How large is that lake?
Let us go down to the landing place.
How much land does your father own?
There is a beautiful lawn in front of the house.
The rooms in that old-fashioned house are very low.
The music is too loud.
We have a large bed of lilies of the valley in our garden.
There are many different kinds of lilies.
What kind of a lily is that?
That is a Calla lily.
My mother raised these lilies from bulbs.
Her first name is Lilian.

(d) Who passed the law?
When was that law passed?
My brother is studying law.
He must ask a lawyer's advice on the subject.
Please buy a spool of linen thread for me.
That linen is too coarse.
I bought a dozen linen handkerchiefs.
My shoes are not large enough.
I must get a larger size.
That is larger than I thought.
It is too late to go today.
"Better late than never."
There was no label on the bottle.
Label all the bottles before you put them on the shelf.
When is Labor Day?
There was no lock on the window.
I have lost my latch-key.
I left my latch-key in the door last night.
This is very poor light.

Our house was struck by lightning last summer.
Who invented the lightning-rod?
Please go to the library and get me a copy of Longfellow's poems.
Where is the Public Library?
Can you tell me the name of the librarian?
There will be a lecture at the library this afternoon.

II. Vocabulary.

Use these words to form new sentences:

NOUNS — lamp, land, law, lake, lark, lily, line, load, loaf, lace, lease, leaf, leaves, lime.

VERBS — learn, lose, look, like, loan, lay, lead, lie.

ADJECTIVES — lame, low, large, long, late.

C — Exercise Story

What are you going to buy?
What are you going to buy on the farm?
What has the farmer to sell?
The farmer sells potatoes.
The farmer sells corn.
The farmer sells wheat.
The farmer sells buckwheat.
Has the farmer any buckwheat to sell?
One day, I went to the farmer to buy some buckwheat.
One day, Mr. Smith went to the farmer to buy some buckwheat for sowing.
How much did he pay?
How much did he wish to buy?
Mr. Smith wanted to buy a bushel.
Mr. Smith wanted to buy four pecks.
One day, Mr. Smith went to the farm to buy a bushel of buckwheat.

Mr. Smith wanted the farmer to sell him four pecks of buckwheat.

The farmer was not at home.

The farmer was not at home, but his wife was there.

The wife undertook to make the sale.

The wife said that she would sell Mr. Smith the buckwheat.

Where did she keep the buckwheat?

She kept the buckwheat in the granary.

She took Mr. Smith to the granary where the buckwheat was kept.

She began to measure the buckwheat.

She found a peck measure.

The farmer's wife filled the peck measure once and poured the contents into a bag.

Then she filled the measure again, and poured the contents into Mr. Smith's bag.

Then she began to tie up the bag.

When Mr. Smith saw her do this....

When Mr. Smith saw her do this, he said, "But, Mrs. Brown, it takes four pecks to make a bushel."

Mrs. Brown did not know that.

She did not know how many pecks it takes to make a bushel.

She did not know how to measure grain.

She told Mr. Smith that she had never measured grain before.

She said, "I never had any experience in measuring grain."

"I never had any experience in measuring grain before I was married."

"I always taught school."

INEXPERIENCED

One day, Mr. Smith went to buy a bushel of buckwheat for sowing. The man who sold the wheat was away, but the wife undertook to make the sale. She found a peck measure, and they went to the granary.

She filled the measure twice, poured the contents into the bag, and began to tie it up.

"But, Mrs. Brown," said the man, "it takes four pecks to make a bushel."

"Oh, does it?" replied the woman, untying the bag. "Well, you see, I never had any experience in measuring grain before I was married. I always taught school."

LESSON XXVI

A

Note. The letter **l** at the end of a word, should have special attention (**oil, awl, hall,** etc.).

Study **l** at the end of a word in sentences under **B.**

B

I. Sentence Practice.

(a) Did you call?
Did they fail?
Did he fall?
Did she tell?
Shall I tell you all about it?
They will call for me.
Call me.
Call for me.
Call for them.
Let me call them up.
Let me call for you.
Let me call him.
Let me call on them.
Be sure to call him on time.
Do not fail to come in here before you leave.
Remember to call for the book at the library.
Leave it at the library.
Do not forget to call them up on the telephone.
Did you call me?
Did you hear that they had called?
If I had time I should call on them.
I cannot call so early.
Did you call their attention to the matter?

I will call his attention to it before I leave.
Do not fail to call their attention to it.

(b) Tell me about it.
Tell the truth.
Tell me what you think.
Tell me all about it.
Tell me the whole story.
Did they sell the house?
He told me that he would like to sell it.
Tell me how you like it.
Would you like to go for a sail on the lake?
Will you mail my letter for me?
Has the mail come?
Seal the letter.
Be sure to seal it before you mail it.
Fill the glass with water.
Fill the bowl with milk.
The cup was full to the brim.
Did you come by rail?
Can you go by rail?
I prefer to go by rail.
How do you spell your name?
Spell it again.
Spell the name for me.
Don't spill the milk.
Be careful not to spill it.
Wait until I come.

(c) That is all there is to say about it.
Pour the oil into the bowl.
The owl is a very wise bird.
Did you go to the ball?
Who rang the bell?
Who paid the bill?
Be sure to boil the water.
The child looks so pale.
"Jack and Jill went up the hill to fetch a pail of water."
Swallow this pill.

That pole is not long enough.
Be careful not to spill the milk.
I am afraid he will spoil the film.
Buy me a spool of blue silk.
The house is for sale.
I wish to sell the old place.
Seal the letter.
The plants stood on the window-sill.
The soil is very fertile.
Are you fond of fried sole?
The sole of my shoe is all worn out.
That is a strange tale.
The fox has a bushy tail.
How tall the boy has grown!
Tell him to wait until tomorrow.

(d) The awl is a carpenter's tool.
This bread is very stale.
The horse was in his stall.
It was made of steel.
Do you think that the boy would steal?
He stole the ring.
It is too cool to sail on the lake.
How much coal do you burn?
The wind was blowing a gale.
What was their goal?
Watch the sea-gull.
This flower grew in a mossy dell.
The evening was very dull.
Come without fail.
How do you feel?
We had a hail storm last night.
The shoe has a high heel.
The hill is steep.
I have torn a hole in my coat.
Bring me my shawl.
Tell the boy to go for the mail.
We live about a mile from the station.
Do you smell the smoke?
How many have you in all.

You have hit the nail on the head.
Did you go by rail?
You must follow the rule.
Will you broil the fish?
I can't read your scrawl.
It would be well for him to go.

II. Vocabulary.

Use these words to form new sentences:

NOUNS — bowl, mole, spool, pool, all, sail, seal, rail, whale, tail, hail, mail, meal, file, tile, mile, oil, coil, soil, curl, awl, hall, ball, wall, well, spell, will, weal, wheel, bell, bill, pill, mill, owl, fowl.

VERBS — spell, spill, fill, feel, fall, sell, tell, mail, boil, soil, toil, fail, call, sail.

ADJECTIVES OR ADVERBS — ill, pale, well, full, tall.

C — Exercise Story

Do you like to go shopping?
Do you ever go shopping alone?
Do you ever ask someone to go with you?
Do you ever ask your wife to go with you?
Were you ever asked by your wife to go shopping?
One day a man was asked by his wife to go shopping.
Where did this man live?
Did he live in town?
Did he live out of town?
Did he live in a suburban town?
Do you live in the suburbs?
I prefer to live in the suburbs.
The man about whom this story is told lived in a suburban town.
One morning....
One morning at Christmas time....

One morning at Christmas time his wife asked him to do something for her.

Will you buy something for me?

Will you buy a book for me?

Will you buy a bag for me?

Will you buy a hat for me?

Will you buy a shirt-waist for me?

Will you please buy a shirt-waist for me when you are in town?

A man who lived in a suburban town was asked by his wife to buy her a shirt-waist.

The man went into a store.

The man went into a department store.

The man went into a department store and asked a saleslady to show him some waists.

What is your favorite color?

Do you like blue?

I like red better than green.

What color do you prefer?

The saleslady asked the man, "What color do you prefer?"

"It does n't make any difference," said the husband.

Choose a pretty one.

Choose anyone of these.

Why did you choose this one?

I like the red one.

"It does n't make any difference," said the husband.

"I believe she would like this one," said the saleslady.

Do you want a large waist?

Do you want a small size?

What size do you wear?

You wear a larger size than I do.

What size did the man want for his wife?

The man said it did n't make any difference.

"It does n't make any difference," was the answer.

"Does n't make any difference?" asked the saleslady.

The saleslady was much surprised to hear that it didn't make any difference what size or color the shirt-waist was to be.

"I should think it would make a great deal of difference!" exclaimed the saleslady.

"Oh, no, it does n't," insisted the wise husband. "No matter what color or what size I got her, I would have to come back tomorrow anyhow and have it exchanged."

WISDOM OF A HUSBAND

A man who lived in a suburban town was asked by his wife to help with the Christmas shopping by buying her a shirt-waist while he was in the city.

Later the saleslady said to him as she displayed a number: "Here are some very pretty ones. What color do you prefer?"

"It does n't make any difference," replied the husband.

"I believe she would like this one," returned the saleslady. "What size do you want?"

"It does n't make any difference," was the surprising answer.

"Does n't make any difference?" exclaimed the wondering saleslady. "I should think it would make a whole lot of difference."

"Oh, no, it does n't!" insisted the wise husband. "No matter what color I got her or what size I got her I would have to come back tomorrow anyhow and have it exchanged."

LESSON XXVII

A

Note. **ge, dge,** and **tch** after a short vowel, have the same movement as **sh** or **ch** in Lesson **XXII.**

Study these in sentences under **B.**

B

I. Sentence Practice.

Catch the ball.
Can you catch it?
Have you a match?
Can you match this silk for me?
That is a good match.
Where is the match-box?
There is not a match in the box.
Did you catch some fish this morning?
Lift up the latch.
There was no latch on the gate.
The latch on our gate is broken.
Have you seen my latch-key?
The boy was working in the potato-patch.
The cat will scratch you.
Do not scratch the table.
Do not scratch your match on the wall.
I saw the boy snatch the apple from the cart.
Have you ever seen a base ball match?
They say he is a fine watch-maker.
Can you patch this for me?

Can you stitch this seam for me?
"A stitch in time saves nine."
Stitch it up on the machine.
Show me how to hem-stitch.
Shall we have a game of bridge?
I will teach you how to play bridge.
When we were in Venice we crossed the "Bridge of Sighs."
When was the "Brooklyn Bridge" built?
The man is very rich.
Which one will you have?
Which bridge did you cross?
Do you like the smell of pitch?
It was pitch dark in the room.
The automobile ran into a ditch.
Which of these books have you read?
I don't remember which one I gave him.
In Salem there is an old witch-house.
My watch has stopped.
The spring in my watch is broken.

Which one of the boys found the watch?
Fetch me the book.
Where is my sketch-book?
Stretch the cloth.
Stretch out your arms.
Can you sketch?
Who taught you how to sketch.
I watched the man sketch the picture.
There is a beautiful hedge around the place.
It is a hawthorn hedge.
How high is the bridge?
The sledge was drawn by the dogs.
He broke the sledge.
The blacksmith uses a sledge hammer.
The man has signed the pledge.
He will pledge ten dollars to the cause.
The judge was in the court-room.
You must not judge the man by his looks.

II. Vocabulary.

Use these words to form new sentences:

NOUNS — catch, latch, patch, match, scratch, notch, lodge, ditch, witch, stitch, switch, ridge, (rich), bridge, hedge, ledge, sledge, wedge, crutch, drudge, fudge.

VERBS — catch, hatch, patch, match, snatch, dodge, pitch, twitch, fetch, stretch, pledge, clutch, judge, budge, grudge.

C — Exercise Story

Once there was a farmer.
Where was the farmer?
What did the farmer do?
The farmer worked in the field.
The farmer sowed some grain.
A farmer had sown his fields with grain.
The farmer was troubled.
The farmer was greatly troubled.
The farmer was much annoyed.
The farmer was vexed.
Why was the farmer vexed?
What troubled the farmer?
The farmer was troubled by some birds.
The farmer was troubled by some crows.
The farmer was troubled by some cranes.
What did the cranes do?
The cranes picked up all the farmer's seeds.
The cranes devoured all the farmer's seeds.

The cranes ate all the farmer's seeds before they had time to grow.

The cranes came and ate all the farmer's seed before it had time to take root.

So the farmer thought....
So the farmer decided.....
So the farmer determined....
So the farmer resolved....

So the farmer made up his mind to get rid of the cranes.
So the farmer determined to free himself from the cranes.
The farmer decided to drive off the cranes.
What did he do?
How did he do it?
How did the get rid of the cranes?
He placed some nets about the fields.
He put a number of nets about the fields.
In this way he caught the cranes.
Thus he captured the cranes.
But what did he find with the cranes?
The farmer found a stork with the cranes.
The farmer found a stork in the net with the cranes.
The stork wanted to run away.
The stork tried to escape.
In trying to escape the stork had broken one of his legs.
While endeavoring to make his escape the stork had broken one of his legs.
The stork said to the farmer.
The stork asked the farmer.
The stork besought the farmer to let him go.
The stork said to the farmer, "Please take pity upon my broken leg."
Please take pity on me.
Please have compassion on me.
Then too....
Then besides....
Moreover....
"Moreover," said the stork, "I am no crane."
"I am a stork."
"I am a good bird."
"I am a bird of good character."
The crane said to the farmer, "Just look at my feathers and you will see that I am no crane."
"Just look at my feathers and you will be convinced that I am no crane."
"My feathers do not resemble those of a crane at all."
The farmer laughed and said, "This may all be true."
"It may be as you say."

The farmer only laughed at the stork and said, "This may all be true, but as I have caught you with the cranes you must suffer with them."

THE FARMER AND THE STORK

Once a farmer had sown his fields with grain. He was very much troubled by some cranes, who ate all seeds before they had time to take root. The farmer determined to free himself from the cranes. He put a number of nets about the fields and in this way he caught the cranes. He found a stork in one of the nets with the crane. The stork had broken one of his legs, in trying to escape. The stork earnestly besought the farmer to let him go. He said, "Please be merciful. Besides I am no crane, but a bird of good character. Look at my feathers and you will be convinced that I am no crane." The farmer laughed and said, "This may be so, but since I have caught you with the cranes, you must suffer with them."

LESSON XXVIII

A

Note. **ch** and **ge** after long vowels have the same movement as **ch** (or **sh**) before a vowel in Lesson **XXII.**

Study these in sentences under **B.**

B

I. Sentence Practice.

We passed through the arch-way.
How high is the arch?
The band played a march.
We saw the soldiers march by.
We shall leave on the fifteenth of March.
The larch is a tree.
It is too large.
That is not large enough.
How much did they charge you for it?
There is too much starch in my waist.
They did not broach the subject.
We watched the train approach.
Will you poach an egg for me?
Did you ever ride in a stage-coach?
The stage will meet you at the station.
The stage passes our house every day.
Have you seen the play on the stage?
There were only three people on the stage.
"All the world's a stage, and all the men and women players."
The man flew into a rage.

Read over the page carefully.
What is the age of the child?
The children are of the same age.
I have copied a page and a half.
The boy was a page.
Turn to page twenty-four.
The bird flew out of its cage.
You must learn each lesson carefully.
I gave each child a peach.
Teach me how to do it.
Can you reach him by telephone?
I shall not urge them to go.
Practice what you preach.
I hope we shall reach the station in time.
I heard him make a speech.
Bleach the cloth.
I would not urge them to go.
My suit is made of blue serge.
The boys caught some perch.
The birch is a useful tree.
It was made of birch-bark.
Please give me one of each kind.
Who will take charge of the work?
Give up the search.

II. Vocabulary.

Use these words to form new sentences:

NOUNS — barge, starch, coach, cage, page, rage, stage, peach, beach, speech, dirge, verge, lurch.

VERBS — march, starch, coach, teach, reach, preach, bleach, screech.

C — Exercise Story

Do you like flowers?
Do you like wild flowers?

I like cultivated flowers.
I like to see flowers in the window.
The florist has flowers in the window.
What kind of flowers has the florist?
Will you buy me a dozen roses at the florist?
Where shall I buy the pinks?
Where shall I buy the azalias?
Where shall I buy the geraniums?
Where shall I buy the begonias?
Where shall I buy the lilies?
The window was full of all kinds of flowers.
One day the florist's window was full of all kinds of flowers.
It was full of bright flowers.
It looked very attractive.

One day the florist's window, full of gay flowers looked unusually attractive.

Many people stopped to look at it.
Some people went into the florist's shop.
One day a woman went into the florist's shop.

One day a woman who looked as if she were determined to have her own way entered the florist's.

She looked at all the flowers.

She looked at the azalias, the geraniums, the begonias and the lilies.

She bought some flowers.
She bought a plant.
One day a woman went into the florist's and selected a plant.
What kind of a plant was it?
It was a brilliant looking plant.
It was a Japanese plant.

Did you see that brilliant looking plant in a Japanese flower-pot?

One day a woman who looked as though she were determined to have her own way entered the florist's shop and selected a brilliant looking plant in a Japanese flower-pot.

How much did she pay for the plant?
She paid the clerk two dollars for the plant.

She paid the clerk for the plant and then she asked him if it would do well in the sun.

"Will that plant do well in the sun?"

"Yes," replied the salesman.

"Yes," replied the salesman, "it will do well in the sun."

The woman said, "Don't say it will if it won't."

"That brilliant looking plant will do well in the sun," replied the man.

Do geraniums do well in the sun?

Do azalias do well in the sun?

Some plants do better in the shade.

Will that brilliant looking plant do better in the shade?

Will the shade hurt it?

The woman in the shop asked, "Will the shade hurt it?"

"Not in the least," replied the clerk.

"Ah," said the woman with a tightening of the lips, "here is a plant that will do equally well in the shade or in the sun."

Will the azalias do equally well in the sun or the shade?

Will the lilies do equally well in the sun or the shade?

Is it probable that those flowers will do equally well in the sun or in the shade?

It is not probable.

It is not natural.

Did the clerk think it was probable or natural?

Did the clerk know?

Did the clerk know anything about botany?

The woman did not think that the clerk was an authority in botany.

The woman said, "Here is a plant that is declared to do equally well in the shade or sun, which, to say the least, is neither probable nor natural."

"Perhaps you will call someone who is more of an authority in botany than yourself."

The young man went into the other rroom.

The young man went away to call his employer.

The employer came in.

The employer came in and spoke to the woman.

The woman told the employer what his assistant had said.

"Your assistant," said the woman, "informs me that this plant does equally well in the shade or sun."

"Well, madam, I think he is right."

The employer said that the clerk was right.

The employer said that the brilliant plant in the Japanese flower-pot would do equally well in the shade or sun.

"Really," said the woman, "that is a most accommodating plant."

"My good sir," said the woman scornfully, "that is really a most accommodating plant. It isn't natural."

"Precisely, madam, You see, it is an artificial plant," said the florist.

AT THE FLORIST'S

The florist's window, full of bright flowers, looked very attractive.

Soon a woman entered who looked as though she were used to having her own way.

She selected a brilliant looking plant in a Japanese flower-pot, and inquired if it would do well in the sun.

"Certainly," said the clerk.

"Don't say it if it won't," she remarked sharply. "Now, if it grows well in the sun, will the shade hurt it?"

"Not in the least," replied the man.

"Ah," said she, with a tightening of the lips, "here is a plant that is declared to do equally well in shade or sun, which to say the least is neither natural nor probable. Perhaps you will call somebody who is more of an authority in botany than yourself."

The young man called his employer.

"Your assistant," said the woman, "informs me that this plant does equally well in shade or sun."

"Well, madam, I think he is right."

"Really, a most accommodating plant," said the woman, scornfully. "My good sir, it isn't natural."

"Precisely, madam. You see, it is an artificial plant."

LESSON XXIX

A

Note 1. The letter **k** (or **ck**) after short vowels, **ă, ŏ, ĭ, ŭ, ĕ,** are to receive special attention in this lesson. We add **oo** (as in book) to this group, it having been omitted in Lesson **XIII** because there are no common words containing **oo** followed by **n.**

Note 2. Pay more attention to the vowels and the consonants preceding them than to the final consonants. The latter are not often seen in rapid conversation and it is really unnecessary to see them. It is far more important to get the right vowel and the consonant preceding.

Study **k** (or **ck**) after short vowels in sentences under **B.**

B

I. Sentence Practice.

Come back.
Bring it back.
Bring back the book.
He brought it back.
My book is black.
Pack the trunk.
How long will it take you to pack your trunk?
What do they lack?
What is in that sack?
My brother's name is Jack.
Crack the ice.

Crack the nuts.
That was a hard nut to crack.
The tramp was walking on the railroad track.
Lock the door.
Knock at the door.
Let us sit down on the rock by the shore.
The farmer has a flock of sheep.
Can you see the clock from here?
The hands of the clock are black.
Look at it.
Look at me.
Look at your book.
She took it away.
She took it back.
She took back the book.
Who took my book?
Can you cook?
Do you like to cook?
Let me look at your cook-book?
Hang your hat on the hook.
There is a hook on the closet door.
The boys have gone fishing in the brook.
Do you like brook-trout?
Jack must bring back the book.
The ship will dock today.
It was a great shock to them.
Has he recovered from the shock?
I bought a book-rack.
How many books are there in the rack?
What luck!
We have had such bad luck.
The house was struck by lightning.
The clock struck twelve.
Pick it up.
Pick up my book.
We must pick a quart of berries.
Can you hear your watch tick?
We played a trick on my brother Jack.
What was the trick?

The wick in the lamp is too short.
The house is made of brick.
The man is a brick-layer.
Put another stick of wood into the fire.
The boy's name is Dick.
That ship has a fine deck.
Have you been out on deck?
There was not a speck of dust in the room.
I want a peck of apples.
How many quarts are there in a peck?

II. Vocabulary.

Use these words to form new sentences:

NOUNS — back, hack, Jack, pack, tack, track, rock, sock, block, clock, shock, book, look, nook, crook, brook, duck, luck, pluck, deck, neck.

VERBS — pack, crack, dock, lock, knock, mock, flock, hook, cook, suck, kick, lick, pick, stick, peck.

C — Exercise Story

Have you ever been to Washington?
Have you ever stopped at a hotel in Washington?
Can you tell me the name of a good hotel there?
Is it a first-class hotel?
It is not far from the station.
Can you direct me to a first-class hotel in the neighborhood of the station?
When did you go to Washington?
How long did you stay?
I went to Washington some time ago and stayed several days.
Once a man from New York went to Washington for several days.
Nobody at the hotel liked the man.

He made himself very much disliked.
He made himself very obnoxious.
He was a very tall man.
He was a large man.
He was a pompous man.
He was a large and pompous person.
He wore a long coat.
He wore a high hat.

Once a large and pompous person, wearing a high hat and a long coat made himself obnoxious around a Washington hotel.

Where did this man live?
This large and pompous person came from New York.
He announced that he was from New York.
He troubled everyone.
He nagged the bell-boys.
He scolded the clerks.
He roared at the food.
He complained about his room.
He complained about the elevator.
He complained about the telephones.
He complained about everything.
One day he called a porter.
One afternoon he called a porter and said, ...
He said, "I'm going to leave this hotel."
He said, "I'm going back to New York."
He said, "I'm going to quit this town."

He said, "I'm going to quit this town and go back to New York where I can get some decent service."

Are you going back to New York?
What train are you going to take?
When does the train leave?
I'm going to take the four o'clock train.
Have you bought your tickets?
How many tickets do you want?
I am going to buy four tickets.
I am going to buy three tickets.
I am going to buy one ticket.
I want a parlor car ticket.
I want a ticket for the Pullman car.

Here are two tickets for the parlor car.

Get me two seats in the parlor car on the four o'clock train.

Meet me at the station.

Meet me at the station with the tickets.

The disagreeable man asked the porter in a Washington hotel to get him some tickets.

He said, "I'm going to quit this town and go back to New York where I can get some decent service. I want you to buy me two seats in a parlor car on the four o'clock train to New York. Get me two seats and meet me at the station with the tickets."

Why did the man want two tickets?

Was someone going with him?

Who was going to accompany him?

Did the man want the porter to go with him?

Was one seat for the disagreeable man and one for the porter?

No, the man wanted both seats for himself.

He wanted one chair to sit it.

He wanted one chair to put his feet in.

He said to the porter, "I want one chair to sit in and one to put my feet in."

The porter went to the station to buy the tickets.

He delivered the tickets to the man.

The seats were delivered.

The seats were delivered at the train.

The seats were delivered at the train just before it pulled out.

The porter delivered the seats at the train just before it pulled out.

One of the seats was in Car No. 3.

The other was located in Car No. 4.

SOMEWHAT OF A STRETCH

A large and pompous person, wearing a high hat and a long coat, for several days made himself obnoxious around a Washington hotel.

He announced he was from New York, nagged the bell-boys, scolded the clerks, roared at the food, complained about his room and the elevator and the telephones and everything else.

One afternoon he called a porter and said, "I'm going to quit this town and go back to New York where I can get some decent service. I want you to buy me two seats in a parlor car on the four o'clock New York train. Get me two seats and meet me at the station with the tickets. I want one chair to sit in and one to put my feet in."

The seats were delivered at the train just before it pulled out. One of the seats was in Car No. 3, and the other was located in Car No. 4.

LESSON XXX

A

Note. **k** (or **ke**) after long vowels and diphthongs have the same movement as **k** (or **ck**) after short vowels in Lesson **XXIX.**

Study these in sentences under **B.**

B

I. Sentence Practice.

Hear the dog bark.
It is so dark.
Have you been to walk in the park?
I should not like to go there alone after dark.
The lark is a bird.
Hark! I hear a lark.
I saw a lark in the park.
Your work is not up to the mark.
He spoke to the man in the park.
I smell the smoke.
That was a good joke.
Tell us the joke.
The boy played the joke on his brother.
Who broke my window?
That is a fine oak tree.
There is a large oak tree in the park.
Hear the frogs croak.
Do you burn coke?
Soak it in water for an hour.
She wore a long black cloak.
Take it with you when you go.

Take it away.
Take the cake with you when you go.
Take it along.
Do it for my sake.
Can you bake good cake?
We had a clam-bake at the sea-shore.
We have been rowing on the lake.
Rake the hay.
I cannot find the rake.
Buy a new rake when you go to town.
Will you wake me at seven?
Were you awake then?
Can you show me how to make it?
I will make it for you.
Make it as long as possible.
Let me take a look at it.
Will you have some steak?
The steak is not cooked enough.
The bird has a sharp beak.
I was there last week.
They arrived a week ago.
Speak to them about it.
That man is a Greek.
There was a leak in the dike.
I should like to go.
Have you ever seen Pike's Peak?
I must finish my work.
My work is done.

II. Vocabulary.

Use these words to form new sentences:

Nouns — lark, park, Clark, toque, cake, lake, flake, peak, freak, dike, Turk, Greek.

Verbs — hark, mark, poke, soak, bake, make, rake, peek, like, work.

C — Exercise Story

Have you ever been abroad?

Have you ever been across the Pacific Ocean?

Have you ever been to Japan?

Japan is a very interesting country.

The Japanese are very interesting people.

The people of Japan are very interesting.

The Japanese are very different from Americans.

Do you know much about Japan?

Do you know anything about the history of Japan?

Do you know anything about the climate of Japan?

There have been a great many earthquakes in Japan.

Earthquakes occur very often in Japan.

Earthquakes occur very often in Japan, but they are not always dangerous.

The people do not think much about them.

The earthquakes are seldom dangerous and the people do not pay much attention to them.

Sometimes....

Sometimes after an earthquake....

Sometimes after an earthquake the sea is very rough.

Sometimes after an earthquake the sea becomes very rough.

The waves are very high.

The waves rise high into the air.

The sea rushes up over the land.

The sea rushes up over the land in the form of a tidal wave.

Sometimes after an earthquake there is a great tidal wave.

The tidal waves are very dangerous.

A great many people have been killed by tidal waves.

A great many towns have been swept away.

Sometimes after an earthquake the sea rushes up over the land in the form of a great tidal wave, which sweeps away whole villages and kills many people...

Once upon a time....

Once upon a time many years ago....

There was a small village in Japan.

There was a small village by the sea in Japan.

About four hundred people lived there.

There were about four hundred inhabitants in the village.

They were all very poor.

They were all very poor but they were very happy and satisfied.

There was only one rich man in the village.

He was very rich.

He was a rich farmer.

He lived on a hill.

His house was on a hill.

His house was on a high hill overlooking the village.

His house was on a high hill overlooking the village by the sea.

Everyone could see the house from the village.

The house could be plainly seen from the village.

The farmer was a very old man.

He had always been a rich man.

He made his money by selling rice.

He had a great many large rice fields.

He had the largest rice fields in the country.

Once upon a time there was a small village of about four hundred inhabitants. They were all very poor, but very happy There was only one rich farmer among them. He lived in a house on the top of the hill, overlooking the village and he owned the largest rice fields in the country.

One day....

One day in the village by the sea....

One day in the village by the sea there was a great festival.

One day a great festival was being held in the village.

All the people went down to the sea-shore.

All the people, men, women, and children, went down to the seashore.

They did not do any work on that day.

They left their work.

They left their work and gathered together to play games.

One day in a village by the sea there was a great festival and all the people, men, women, and children, gathered together to play games.

Everyone was there.

Everyone in the village was there except the rich farmer.

Everyone was there except the rich farmer and his little grandson.

The old man had been very ill.

The old man had been very ill and so he could not go to the festival.

The little boy stayed with him.

The little boy stayed with him to keep him company.

They were both sitting in front of the house.

They were both sitting in front of the house on the hill.

They were sitting at the top of the hill watching the people.

They were sitting there watching the people in the village below.

Suddenly.....

All of a sudden....

All of a sudden there came an earthquake.

It was not a very severe one.

It was not a very severe one and the people did not pay any attention to it.

The people did not pay any attention to the earthquake but went on with their games.

After the earthquake, the sea grew very calm.

After the earthquake, the sea grew very still.

The old man was watching it.

He thought the sea looked very strange.

The sea seemed very strange.

The sea seemed to be moving slowly.

The sea seemed to be running away from the land.

The people saw it too.

The people watched it for a while.

The people watched it for a while and then went on with their games.

The sea crept slowly away.

The sea crept slowly away from the land.

The old man arose from his seat.

The old man arose quickly from his seat.

He arose quickly from his seat and called his grandson.

He called his grandson and told him to light a torch.

He called his grandson and told him to bring a lighted torch.

The child obeyed.

The child hastened to obey.

The child hastened to obey and the old man took the torch.

The old man took the torch and began to run towards the rice fields.

He began to set fire to the rice.

He ran to set fire to the rice fields.

He ran from one field to another until he had set fire to all the rice.

The little boy began to cry.

The little boy began to cry for he thought that his grandfather had gone crazy.

The people in the village saw the fire.

They rang a bell.

They rang the fire alarm.

They rang the fire alarm and then they ran up the hill.

They all ran up the hill as fast as they could.

They all ran up the hill as fast as they could to help put out the fire.

The men came first.

First came the men, then the women and children.

The women and children all followed the men.

When the first ones came up the hill they started to put out the fire.

They immediately started to put out the fire.

Immediately they began to put out the fire but the old man would not let them.

He would not let them put out the fire.

They thought he had gone crazy.

When all the people had come up the hill the old man pointed to the sea.

They all looked towards the sea.

The sea was very terrible.

It was not moving away from the land now.

It was coming towards the land.

A great wave was coming towards the land.

A great wave as high as a mountain was coming towards the land.

It struck the shore.

It swept over the shore.

It swept over the village.

It swept over the village and then drew back.

When it drew back....

When it drew back the village was gone.

When it drew back the village was gone and there was not a house left.

Again the wave came rushing over the land.

Five times it came rushing over the land.

Five times it came rushing over the land and then it drew back and the sea raged.

Then the old man spoke to the poeple.

Then the old man said to the poeple, "That was why I set fire to the rice."

He said, "Now you know why I set fire to my rice fields."

The rice was all gone.

The rice was all burned.

The rice was all burned and he was a poor man.

He was as poor as any man in the village.

He was as poor as any man in the village but he had saved four hundred lives.

THE EARTHQUAKE AND THE GREAT WAVE

It was an autumn evening more than a hundred years ago. In a little village of Japan there was a great stir. The narrow streets were full of people who were getting ready for a merry making in the evening. Each was thinking how happy he should be in the gay throng.

The village was on the sea-shore. The waves breaking on the beach were only a few feet away. Above, on the high plain behind the village, an old man was watching from his house the merry crowd below.

Suddenly in the midst of the fun and laughter there came the shock of an earthquake. Japan is the land of earthquakes, and this was not enough to frighten anyone.

The boys and girls ran up and down the streets as before. The old man could hear their gay, childish voices. He stood up and looked at the sea. The water was dark and acted strangely. It seemed to be moving against the wind. The sea was running away from the land. Below him, the people were wondering what that great ebb could mean. They were watching it from the beach.

The old man knew what it meant; he knew the danger that was coming. His one thought was to warn the people in the village.

"Bring me a torch! Make haste!" he called to his little grandson. In the fields behind him lay his great crop of rice. It was piled up in stacks ready for the market. It was worth a fortune. The old man hurried out with his torch. In a moment the dry stalks were blazing. The big bell pealed from the temple.

Back from the beach, away from that strange sea, up the steep side of the cliff, came the people of the village. They were coming to try to save the crops of their rich neighbor. They said, "He is mad!"

"Look!" shouted the old man at the top of his voice, as they reached the plain in safety.

They looked eastward through the twilight. At the edge of the horizon they saw a long, lean, dim line, — a line that thickened as they gazed. That line was the sea, rising up like a high wall, and coming more swiftly than a kite flies.

Then came a shock, heavier than thunder. The great swell struck the shore with a weight that sent a shudder through the hills. There was a foam-burst like a blaze of sheet lightning.

When the people looked again, they saw a white horror of sea raging over the place of their homes. It drew back, roaring. Then it struck again, and again, and yet again. Once more it struck and ebbed; then it returned to its place.

On the plain no word was spoken. Of all the homes, only two straw roofs could be seen, tossing on the waves. Then the voice of the old man was heard, saying gently, "That is why I set fire to the rice."

He stood among them almost as poor as the poorest, for his wealth was gone; — but he had saved four hundred lives by the sacrifice.

LAFCADIO HEARN,
Adapted.

PART THREE

Exercises on important initial and final syllables.

Note. The following exercises are given for advanced work when all the preceding lessons have been thoroughly mastered. They consist of phrases and sentences, and are to be practiced as the sentences under **B,** and not with the mirror.

ing

(a) Without mak**ing** a mistake...
Without ask**ing** any questions...
Both com**ing** and go**ing**...
Wait**ing** for a car...
Walk**ing** up the street...
A very amus**ing** remark...
Look**ing** forward...
Mak**ing** the most of it...
Mak**ing** the best of it...
Speak**ing** the truth...
Read**ing** the newspaper...
Writ**ing** the letter...
Mak**ing** many improvements...
Seiz**ing** the opportunity...
Bear**ing** the burden...
Keep**ing** up...
Try**ing** to learn...
Lead**ing** the way...
Read**ing** the report...

Striv**ing** to do one's best...
Mov**ing** about...

(b) While she was read**ing** the newspaper, I was writ**ing** the letter.
They have been think**ing** about it for some time.
What have you been do**ing** this morn**ing?**
I have been writ**ing** letters all morn**ing.**
My sister has been amus**ing** the children.
She told them an amus**ing** story.
The child made some very amus**ing** remarks.
The boy is always ask**ing** questions.
We are all tired of hear**ing** about it.
We have been look**ing** forward to the event for some time.
I have been look**ing** all over the house for you.
Have you been wait**ing** for me?
They have been mak**ing** some improvements in the house.
They are mak**ing** plans for the summer.
Are you com**ing** with me?
I saw her stand**ing** at the corner wait**ing** for a car.

ment

(a) A great disappoint**ment**...
Make an appoint**ment**...
Fulfill the require**ment**...
Reply to the advertise**ment**...
An interesting experi**ment**...
A remarkable achieve**ment**...
Read the announce**ment**...
A reliable state**ment**...
Come to an agree**ment**...
Offer some induce**ment**...
Pay a compli**ment**...
Announce the engage**ment**...
Inflict the punish**ment**...

A large depart**ment** store...
Not in the agree**ment**...
According to the agree**ment**...
Laying the pave**ment**...
Read the supple**ment**...
A doubtful compli**ment**...
Rent the apart**ment**...
Manage**ment** of the business...

(b) Have you any engage**ment** for tomorrow?
I have an appoint**ment** at the dentist's.
Have you read the announce**ment** in the paper?
The advertise**ment** was in the New York paper.
What is your favorite amuse**ment?**
He has been appointed by the govern**ment.**
The govern**ment** will pass the law.
Have you tried the experi**ment?**
What if the experi**ment** fails?
The experi**ment** has proved successful.
Do you remember having read the announce**ment?**
Do you think he deserves the punish**ment?**
The punish**ment** was too severe.
In olden times they wrote on parch**ment.**
The pay**ment** must be made on the first of every month.
I read the announce**ment** of their engage**ment** in the paper.
There was a large assort**ment** of goods displayed in the window.
Where did they rent the apart**ment?**
Did they come to an agree**ment?**
It will be a great disappoint**ment** to them if they are obliged to give up their trip.

er

(a) Bett**er** than nothing...
The more the bett**er**...
Bett**er** late than nev**er**...

Long**er** than usual...
Bett**er** than I thought...
Nev**er** too late to mend...
Near**er** than you think...
An interesting speak**er**...
At anoth**er** time...
The larg**er** the bett**er**...
Furth**er** off...
Few**er** than ev**er**...
Wat**er** the flowers...
Pap**er** the room...
More than ev**er**...
Forev**er** and ev**er**...
Wheth**er** or not it is so...
Deliv**er** the goods...
An enthusiastic admir**er**...
A brave command**er**...
A thoughtful read**er**...
Consid**er** the plan...

(b) My room is much small**er** than yours.
She would rath**er** remain at home.
That is larg**er** than it should be.
The pen is mighti**er** than the sword.
Since I would rath**er** remain at home, why do you urge me to go?
Since it rains, we had bett**er** remain at home.
How much bett**er** it would be if they told her about it at once.
How much long**er** do you intend to stay in town?
As soon as the weath**er** is warm**er** we shall go into the country.
You will find the oth**er** book in the library.
It will nev**er** do to send it by mail.
Did you ev**er** read any of his works?
He is a man of strong charact**er**.
We met both her fath**er** and her broth**er**.
Please write your address on a piece of pap**er**.
You must ent**er** by that door.
You must consid**er** the matt**er** carefully.

We shall do whatev**er** you say.
That was bett**er** than I thought.

ful

(a) Faith**ful** in small things...
A success**ful** enterprise...
A cheer**ful** disposition...
A power**ful** speech...
A wonder**ful** discovery...
A respect**ful** reply...
A delight**ful** evening...
A skil**ful** piece of work...
A beauti**ful** picture...
A faith**ful** servant...
The right**ful** owner...
A plenti**ful** supply...
A joy**ful** occasion...
A disgrace**ful** affair...
A use**ful** article...
A tact**ful** reply...
A hope**ful** outlook...
A delight**ful** evening...
Be care**ful**...
Be truth**ful**...
Be grate**ful**...
Be joy**ful**...
Be cheer**ful**...
Be respect**ful**...

(b) You must be care**ful** not to make such a mistake again.
A telephone is very use**ful.**
Have you seen the beauti**ful** paintings at the Art Museum?
That was indeed a wonder**ful** story.
The undertaking was not altogether success**ful.**
Be care**ful,** I am afraid you will fall.
It seems doubt**ful** whether or not we can go.
That is the most beauti**ful** house on the street.

That man is a very skil**ful** artist.
That was a skil**ful** piece of work.
Fruit is very plenti**ful** this year.
Your friend has a very cheer**ful** disposition.
What do you consider the most wonder**ful** discovery?
Oranges are not very plenti**ful** this year.

tion

(a) A very small por**tion**...
A very valuable collec**tion**...
The introduc**tion** to the book...
A rock forma**tion**...
A mere frac**tion**...
Feel the vibra**tion**...
Like the sensa**tion**...
Perpetual mo**tion**...
Without any hesita**tion**...
Without any explana**tion**...
By way of illustra**tion**...
Reliable informa**tion**...
A solid founda**tion**...
Take part in the conversa**tion**...
Make a sugges**tion**...
A large propor**tion**...
The chief attrac**tion**...
Accept the posi**tion**...
A queer sensa**tion**...
Inspira**tion** of the moment...
Receive a good educa**tion**...
Under great obliga**tion**...
In the wrong direc**tion**...
A vivid imagina**tion**...
A letter of introduc**tion**...
Receive an honorable men**tion**...
Apply for the situa**tion**...
Take up a collec**tion**...
The law of gravita**tion**...
Resist the tempta**tion**...

A good loca**tion**...
Make a transla**tion**...
The history of the Reforma**tion**...

(b) We must not men**tion** this to him.
Can you give me any informa**tion?**
I will give you a letter of introduc**tion** to him.
Have you read the introduc**tion** to the book?
The introduc**tion** was very well written.
In which direc**tion** are you going?
The publica**tion** of the article caused a great sensa**tion.**
What time did you go the sta**tion?**
How long does it take to drive to the sta**tion?**
Did you get any reliable informa**tion** from him?
Do you think he will accept the posi**tion?**
I should like to read a transla**tion** of that book.
Have you made a transla**tion?**
Since you can read the book in French you should not read the transla**tion.**
The newspaper article did not men**tion** his name.
When the time comes you must make a selec**tion.**
Have you seen the beautiful collec**tion** of paintings?
That is a fine loca**tion** for the new club-house.

ist

(a) A famous natura**list**...
An eminent scien**tist**...
A reliable drug**gist**...
A famous specia**list**...
A great American humo**rist**...
Pessi**mist** or opti**mist**...
The American nove**list**...
A well-known natura**list**...

(b) That man is a famous ar**tist.**
Can you tell me the name of the ar**tist** who painted that picture?

I have been to the dent**ist** this morning.
How often do you go to the dent**ist?**
He will consult a special**ist.**
Who is the organ**ist** in your church?
Who is the greatest American humor**ist?**
He is the greatest German novel**ist** of the day.
Can you tell me who is to be the pian**ist** at the next concert?
There was a fine solo**ist** at the concert last evening.
What drugg**ist** do you patronize?
The lecture by the scient**ist** was very instructive.
The audience was very attentive to what the natural**ist** said.
Can you give me the name of a reliable drugg**ist?**

ly

(a) Complete**ly** worn out...
Material**ly** different...
Especial**ly** good...
Great**ly** surprised...
Hard**ly** possible...
Apparent**ly** wrong...
Recent**ly** published...
Remarkab**ly** interesting...
Hard**ly** worth while...
Exact**ly** what I wanted...
Walk very rapid**ly**...
Ear**ly** to bed, ear**ly** to rise...
General**ly** speaking...
Careful**ly** planned...
Real**ly** well done...
Plain**ly** visible...
Arrive punctual**ly**...
Face the situation calm**ly**...
Not exact**ly** right...
Practical**ly** the same...
Leave very ear**ly**...

(b) Do you read the daily paper?
Come as early as possible.
Do that as quickly as possible.
There is only one thing to do.
I hardly believe that she will come so early.
I was greatly surprised to hear of that.
The book was recently published.
The new book is remarkably interesting.
The work was really well done.
The boy always arrived punctually.
Te left the room quietly.
They are usually at home in the evening.
We were cordially invited.
She left instantly without a moment's delay.
I hardly believe that that can be true.
She is especially interested in that line of work.
That is a lovely road, but is very lonely.
I shall certainly come on Monday, if I can.
We shall start early tomorrow morning.
It will hardly be worth while to go for such a short time.

age

(a) Mail the package...
Repair the damage...
Forward the baggage...
A foreign language...
In cold storage...
A high percentage...
Deliver the package...
In a country village...
A message to Congress...
Play a game of cribbage...
During the marriage ceremony...
On an average...
At a great disadvantage...
Telephone for the carriage...

Study the langu**age**...
Check the bagg**age**...
Keep up cour**age**...
Pay for the dam**age**...
Sew on the selv**age**...
Paste it with mucil**age**...
Prepay the post**age**...

(b) Did you receive the pack**age?**
Will you take this pack**age** to the post-office for me?
How much will the post**age** be?
The cott**age** stood back from the road and was almost covered by the foli**age.**
The plum**age** of the tropical birds is often very brilliant.
The foli**age** in any mountains is beautiful in October.
Can she speak any foreign langu**age?**
You must take advant**age** of every opportunity to practice.
They have just bought a new carri**age.**
We drove to the station in a carri**age.**
The President sent his mess**age** to Congress.
It requires a good deal of cour**age** to do that.
Will you buy some mucil**age** for me?
Did you have the bagg**age** checked?
The storm has caused much dam**age** to the trees.
Will you telephone for the carri**age?**
We spent the summer in a small country vill**age.**
Did you prepay the post**age** on the pack**age?**
We were at a great disadvant**age** from the beginning.

ive

(a) A progress**ive** whist party...
A very impress**ive** sermon...
A fest**ive** occasion...
In the superlat**ive** degree...
A sensit**ive** child...

A posit**ive** statement...
Altogether too expens**ive**...
In a reflect**ive** mood...
A descript**ive** passage...
A private detect**ive**...
A very attent**ive** listener...
The exclus**ive** privilege...
The exclus**ive** right...
Posit**ive** or negat**ive**...

(b) I hope you will be very attent**ive** to what he says.
He is always attent**ive.**
She is very sensit**ive** about the matter.
That is altogether too expens**ive.**
She is very act**ive.**
I am posit**ive** that the boy had nothing to do with the affair.
She is a relat**ive** of mine.
How expens**ive** is the house?
The ceremony was very impress**ive.**
He made a very impress**ive** speech.
The lectures have been very instruct**ive.**
Can you name three interrogat**ive** pronouns?
The fire proved very destruct**ive.**
He leads an act**ive** life.
Have you ever been to a progress**ive** whist-party?
There was an interesting detect**ive** story in the magazine this month.

able ible

(a) A favor**able** decision...
A respons**ible** position...
A reason**able** price...
A sens**ible** remark...
A remark**able** coincidence...
An agree**able** surprise...
A profit**able** investment...
Respons**ible** for the loss...

A favor**able** impression...
A reli**able** statement...
The invari**able** rule...
An agree**able** sensation...
The prob**able** outcome...
A desir**able** situation...
An irresist**ible** attraction...
An accept**able** gift...
An admir**able** arrangement...
A navig**able** river...
Any reli**able** information...
A horr**ible** accident...
A terr**ible** catastrophe...

(b) That is a very prob**able** explanation.
I hope you will find your room comfort**able.**
The whole affair is quite incomprehens**ible.**
They have had consider**able** trouble about the matter.
The pupil must repeat each syll**able.**
It seems to be the invari**able** rule.
The man was knocked insens**ible** by the blow.
We will mark the linen with indel**ible** ink.
She will hold you respons**ible** for it.
If it is agree**able** to you, I will go with you.
Her sister is a most cap**able** person.
The facts of the story do not seem very prob**able.**
It is very prob**able** that I shall go.
The weather has been very disagree**able.**
Can you give me some reli**able** information?
He is a very reli**able** man.
She holds a respons**ible** position.

ance ence

(a) Learn by experi**ence**...
Notice the differ**ence**...
Show a prefer**ence**...
The persever**ance** that wins...
An interesting correspond**ence**...

A large confer**ence**...
Change your resid**ence**...
Self-reli**ance**...
Make the acquaint**ance**...
A struggle for exist**ence**...
Considerable influ**ence**...
A life insur**ance** company...
Differ**ence** of opinion...
Complete sil**ence**...
A great conveni**ence**...
Pres**ence** of mind...
A long dist**ance** telephone...

(b) There is a strong family resembl**ance** among the children.
The entr**ance** to the hotel is on the other street.
It requires pati**ence** and persever**ance** to do the work well.
He showed great pres**ence** of mind.
He has considerable influ**ence** in the town.
A telephone is a great conveni**ence.**
I should be glad to make their acquaint**ance.**
There was a complete sil**ence** in the room when she entered.
Have you any prefer**ence?**
Did you attend the confer**ence?**
Did you notice the differ**ence?**
That makes no differ**ence** to me.
There was a great differ**ence** of opinion in the matter.
Has he had any experi**ence** in that kind of work?

con

(a) **Con**fess the truth...
Confirm the report...
Consult a physician...
Contradict the report...
The **con**tinuation of the story...
Contrary to my expectations...

Condemn the criminal...
Strictly **con**fidential...
Entirely too **con**spicuous...
Conspire against the government...
Concentrate one's thoughts...
A large **con**tribution...
Continual interruptions...
A **con**cise statement...
Confiscate the goods...
A large **con**flagration...
A **con**genial companion...
A **con**scientious worker...
Make **con**nections...
In a very good **con**dition...
Consider it seriously...
Conduct the services...

(b) I will go with you upon one **con**dition.
I will never **con**sent to such an arrangement.
The prisoner was **con**demned to death.
That **con**firms my suspicions.
The article must be **con**densed before it is published.
We tried to **con**vince him of the importance of the matter.
She will never give her **con**sent.
Do you know what that box **con**tains?
We must **con**trive some good way to carry out our plans.
How long does the work **con**tinue?
We must **con**gratulate them upon their good fortune.
I will come at any time that is **con**venient for you.
The book must be returned in good **con**dition.
They came very early, **con**trary to my expectations.
I wish to read the **con**tinuation of the story.

sub

(a) **Sub**merged by the waves...
Subtract the remainder...

A **sub**urban residence...
An interesting **sub**ject...
The **sub**stance of the report...
Subscribe to the paper...
A problem in **sub**traction...
Change the **sub**ject...
A **sub**terranean passage...
Sublet the apartment...
Subdue the revolt...
A **sub**ordinate officer...
The **sub**sequent events...
Submit to authority...

(b) What was the **sub**ject of the lecture?
What was the **sub**stance of the report?
The general gave orders to his **sub**ordinate officers.
Does this car go through the **sub**way?
The **sub**ject of the debate is very interesting.
They are trying to find a **sub**stitute to fill the place.
Can you tell me the **sub**sequent results?
You must **sub**tract that from the amount received.
They have bought a new house in the **sub**urbs.
Have you **sub**scribed to the paper?
Shall you continue your **sub**scription to the magazine?
We were delayed in the **sub**way.
Let us change the **sub**ject.
We will try to **sub**let the apartment.

in

(a) An **in**appropriate remark...
An **in**convenient time...
A strong **in**clination...
An **in**finite number...
The **in**evitable result...
An important **in**vention...
An educational **in**stitution...
Increase in value...
An **in**delible impression...

A strong **in**clination...
Offer some **in**ducement...
An **in**telligent reply...
Indefinitely postponed...
The Declaration of **In**dependence...
An **in**describable sensation...
A strong **in**dividuality...
A profitable **in**vestment...
Inherit the property...
Innumerable faults...
An **in**considerate remark...
Inseparable playmates...
An **in**correct statement...

(b) Can you give me any **in**formation on the subject?
Will you please **in**form him of the change in our plans?
She shows much **in**terest in her work.
Did he **in**troduce the subject?
We mean to **in**form them of our plans.
What ever **in**duced her to say such a thing?
The house must be **in**sured against fire.
When do they **in**augurate the President of the United States.
Have you found the title in the **in**dex?
Owing to a previous engagement we shall not be able to accept the **in**vitation.
I am **in**clined to think she will return.
Does that **in**clude everything?
He was very **in**dignant when he heard about it.
The new book seems to be very **in**teresting.
How many **in**habitants has the town?
Is there an **in**dex to the book?

pre

(a) A wise **pre**caution...
A **pre**liminary step...
A **pre**vious engagement...
A **pre**meditated crime...

Prepay the postage...
Preside at the meeting...
A **pre-**historic animal...
A **pre-**occupied state of mind...
Prevent the catastrophe...
The **pre**vailing fashion...
Always well **pre**pared...
Full of **pre**sumption...
Preserve the fruit...
Prescribe the medicine...
To exercise **pre**caution...
The doctrine of **pre-**destination...

(b) Which of these pictures do you **pre**fer?
I wish to **pre**pay the express on that package.
An ounce of **pre**vention is worth a pound of cure.
The work was carefully **pre**pared.
You must be more **pre**cise in your statements.
I **pre**sume that she will join us later.
You must **pre**tend that you know nothing about it.
Ask the doctor to **pre**scribe something for your cold.
You can have the **pre**scription made up at the drug-store.
We cannot accept because of a **pre**vious engagement.
Who is to **pre**side at the next meeting?
I **pre**sume that they will go abroad in the fall.
They used every **pre**caution, but it was of no use.
He belongs to the Society for the **Pre**vention of Cruelty to Animals.

mis

(a) Recognize the **mis**take...
A great **mis**fortune...
Misplaced confidence...
A **mis**print in the book...
Miscalculate the time...
Misdirect the letter...
Mistakes will happen...

Met with a **mis**hap...
Misfortunes never come singly...
Mispronunciation of the word...
Misinterpret the passage...
Misrepresent the facts...
Misunderstand the message...

(b) Are you sure that you did not **mis**understand what he told you?
I think you have made a great **mis**take.
That was indeed a great **mis**fortune.
She has **mis**spelled several words in her letter.
He **mis**placed the book and could not find it.
You **mis**apply the meaning of his remarks.
The children were always up to some **mis**chief.
She is so apt to **mis**represent.
You have surely **mis**judged them.
The article was very **mis**leading.
There must have been some **mis**take in the account.
The letter was **mis**sent.
There were a great many **mis**takes in the lesson.
She seemed to **mis**trust that something would happen.

ad

(a) **Ad**journ the meeting...
The most **ad**vanced pupil...
Adapt one's self to circumstances...
A few **ad**ditional remarks...
In spite of **ad**versity...
Advertise in the paper...
Adjust the matter...
Adopt the child...
Take **ad**vantage of the offer...
Give some good **ad**vice...
The **ad**ministrator of the estate...
The price of **ad**mission...
No **ad**mittance...
An **ad**vantageous offer...

(b) I think the matter can be **ad**justed with very little trouble.
I hope you will **ad**here to your resolution.
What is the price of **ad**mission?
He is to deliver an **ad**dress at the next meeting.
We must **ad**just the book-shelves to make them the right height.
He can give you valuable **ad**vice upon the matter.
They told us about a most interesting **ad**venture.
I saw the **ad**vertisement in the morning paper.
The stamp will not **ad**here to the envelope.
No child will be **ad**mitted who is not accompanied by an **ad**ult.
They are building an **ad**dition to the house.
What would you **ad**vise me to do?

ab

(a) An **ab**solute fact...
An **ab**surd statement...
Abbreviate the word...
An **ab**undance of fruit...
An **ab**ridged edition...
Abrupt departure...
Absurd undertaking...
An **ab**sorbing subject...
An **ab**undant supply...
Abolish the custom...
Abolition of slavery...
Absolutely no time...
Absent minded...
Absolutely necessary...
Above suspicion...
Absolution of sin...

(b) There is **ab**solutely no reason why you should not go.
In taking notes try to **ab**breviate as many words as possible.

His answer was rather **ab**rupt but it was to the point.
The children have been **ab**sent from school a great deal.
The prisoner was **ab**solved from guilt and set free at once.
Did you read the **ab**stract from the article that was published in the paper?
What an **ab**surd idea.
We have **ab**solutely no time to spare.
Are you going **ab**road this summer?
No, we have **ab**andoned the idea.
How much will the **ab**ridged edition of the encyclopedia cost?
When was slavery **ab**olished?

pro

(a) **Pro**nounce the word...
Proficient in the art...
A **pro**fusion of flowers...
A **pro**vincial town...
The **pro**bate court...
The **pro**bation officer...
An interesting **pro**ceeding...
The **pro**prietor of the hotel...
Procrastination is the thief of time...
Proclaim the good tidings...
A **pro**ductive soil...
Progressive whist...
A **pro**gram of the play...
Prohibit the sale...
Proceed with care...
Provide for an emergency...
A **pro**found silence...
Profuse thanks...
Provided that is so...
Follow the **pro**cession...
Receive **pro**motion...
Before the **pro**bate court...

(b) Can you tell me how to **pro**nounce this word?
The **pro**cession will start at three o'clock.
Peace was **pro**claimed throughout the country.
One of the students was put on **pro**bation.
We must **pro**ceed with the work just the same.
We had a good view of the **pro**cession from our window.
They were unable to **pro**cure the medicine at the country store.
That gentleman is a **pro**fessor of modern languages.
The **pro**gram for the next concert is very fine.
They have made a law to **pro**tect the birds.
We must **pro**vide for them in some way.
It was placed before the **pro**bate court.
Have you read the **pro**logue of the play?
She has become very **pro**ficient in the art.

im

(a) **Im**prove your time...
Very **im**probable...
Utterly **im**possible...
Impatiently waiting...
A matter of grave **im**portance...
Imperative orders...
Imagine all sorts of things...
An **im**prudent remark...
An **im**aginative child...
No **im**mediate danger...
The **im**mortality of the soul...
An **im**perceptible change...
An indelible **im**pression...
Imprisonment for life...
An **im**promptu speech...
A noticeable **im**provement...
Impartial judgment...
From time **im**memorial...
A good **im**pression...

Immaculate order...
Impertinent reply...

(b) It is very **im**portant that this letter should go **im**mediately.
It will be **im**possible to finish the work on time.
That is a very **im**probable story.
The equator is an **im**aginary line.
The change was almost **im**perceptible.
The photograph was **im**perfect.
The king was wearing his **im**perial robes.
Her remarks were quite **im**personal.
There has been a large **im**portation of silk from Japan.
It was a very **im**prudent thing for him to do.
It is utterly **im**possible for me to do that.

com

(a) **Com**pare the different parts...
Commemorate the event...
A **com**mendable resolution...
Receive a **com**mission...
A **com**plicated piece of work...
Comparatively easy...
A few **com**monplace remarks...
A **com**plete failure...
A **com**plimentary remark...
Comply with the request...
Compose the music...
A **com**pound fracture...
Compute the interest...
A great **com**poser...
Without **com**parison...
Receive a **com**pensation...
Filled with **com**passion...
Comprehend the meaning...
A **com**mon mistake...
Appoint a **com**mittee...
Commerical value...
Commit to memory...

(b) They have appointed a **com**mittee of three to report on the matter.
She **com**bines the colors very well.
Will you walk across the **Com**mon with me?
She is on the arrangement **com**mittee.
It is not fair to **com**pare the two.
You must put a **com**ma in that sentence.
The work **com**prises many volumes.
Can you tell me who the **com**poser of that piece is?
You have no reason to **com**plain.
They will **com**plete the work very soon.
Something seemed to **com**pel me to go.
My sister is a **com**petent housekeeper.
It was **com**paratively easy to arrange the matter.
At what time did you **com**mence your lesson?
I am afraid it was a **com**plete failure.

ex

(a) An interesting **ex**periment...
Without any **ex**ception...
An **ex**pensive article...
Expelled from school...
Explain the mistake...
Explicit directions...
Explore the land...
Altogether too **ex**travagant...
An **ex**cellent performance...
A delightful **ex**cursion...
From one **ex**treme to another...
Learn by **ex**perience...
Extensive preparations...
An **ex**pedition to the North Pole...
Set an **ex**ample...
Exceedingly difficult...
Extremely interesting...
Excessively warm...
Pass the **ex**amination...

Exhaust the subject...
An **ex**tract from the book...

(b) I can go any day **ex**cept Thursday.
The cost must not **ex**ceed ten dollars.
You must set the children a good **ex**ample.
Did the boy pass in his **ex**aminations?
She is very **ex**travagant.
They have gone on an **ex**cursion.
Have you seen the **ex**hibition at the Art Club?
Did you go to the St. Louis or the Chicago **ex**position?
I wish to send this package by **ex**press.
Will you **ex**plain the lesson to me?
She uttered an **ex**clamation of surprise when she saw them.
We saw an **ex**cellent performance at the theatre yesterday.
It has been **ex**cessively warm this summer.
The lecture was **ex**tremely interesting.
We had a great deal of **ex**tra work to do.
The boy was **ex**pelled from school last year.
That is too **ex**pensive.
The comma and **ex**clamation point are marks of punctuation.

dis

(a) **Dis**appear from view...
Disapprove of the plan...
Much to my **dis**may...
About to be **dis**missed...
Disbelieve the report...
Discard the plan altogether...
Discontinue the subscription...
Make a **dis**tinction...
An interesting **dis**cussion...
Disregard the rights of others...
Distribute the mail...

At a great **dis**advantage...
Discharge the servant...
Sell at a **dis**count...
In great **dis**order...
A wonderful **dis**covery...
A **dis**creet reply...
Discriminate between the two...
Disobey the order...
Disbelieve the story...

(b) That will be a great **dis**appointment to them.
Why did they **dis**charge the man?
Why did you **dis**continue your subscription to the paper?
When did you **dis**cover the mistake?
He refuses to **dis**cuss the subject any more.
How do you **dis**pose of your old magazines?
It is hard to **dis**tinguish one shade from another by this poor light.
The room was in great **dis**order.
She is **dis**satisfied with the result of the work.
The house is quite a long **dis**tance from the car-line.
When is the mail **dis**tributed at the post-office?
What do you consider the most useful **dis**covery?
I think we will **dis**card the plan altogether.
I hope he will not **dis**appoint us.
You were at a **dis**advantage from the first.

en

(a) Receive **en**couragement...
Look it up in the **en**cyclopedia...
Enforce the law...
Endeavor to do better...
Enlarge the house...
An **en**joyable **en**tertainment...
Beyond **en**durance...
Announce the **en**gagement...

Engrave the silver...
With great **en**thusiasm...
An **en**dless piece of work...
The **en**trance to the building...

(b) The garden was **en**closed by a high wall.
The daily practice will **en**able you to do better.
We must **en**deavor to finish the book this evening.
She is very **en**ergetic.
I hope you will **en**joy your trip to Switzerland this summer.
They **en**tertain a great deal.
Did you go to the **en**tertainment last evening?
The **en**tire plan has been given up.
Has the **en**gagement been announced?
They began the work with great **en**thusiasm.
The **en**trance to the house is on the other street.
They intend to **en**large their house next year.
You are to be **en**vied.

EXERCISES ON WORD DEVELOPMENT

A. Subject

SHIP

B. Word Development

ship	shipper
shipping	shipshape
shipped	ship's-papers
shipboard	shipwreck
ship-building	shipyard
ship-chandler	shipment
ship-load	hardship
shipmate	friendship
ship-owner	steamship
warship	airship

C. Conversational Practice

Where was the ship?
What is the name of the ship?
Where was the fruit shipped?
Speak to the shipper.
Have you heard about the shipwreck?
What is a ship-chandler?
How did you spend your time on shipboard?
She left everything in shipshape order.
Did you go on board the new ship?
Did you say that the ship was due today?
A great deal of shipping is carried on on the Great Lakes.
The fruit was shipped from the south in crates.
We passed many pleasant hours on shipboard.
A ship-load of bananas has just arrived from the south.
You will find the canvas at the ship-chandler's.
The shipper made a mistake which caused a delay in shipping the goods.

The goods are all ready for shipment.
Have you ever visited any of the large shipbuilding yards of Europe?
Everything was left in shipshape order.
The ship will leave port as soon as the ship's papers are filled.
The early settlers endured many hardships.
Did you ever go on board a warship?
Would you like to cross the ocean in an airship?
Ask the clerk at the steamship office what time the ship is due.
The goods must be shipped at once.
The boys were shipmates on a cruise around the world.
How did you pass the time on board the ship?
Where did you see the airship?
Their friendship dates back many years.

A. Subject

AIR

B. Word Development

air	air-cushion
airs	airship
airing	air-thermometer
airily	air-tight
air-castle	air-pump
National air	air-plant
	air-shaft

C. Conversational Practice

Air the room.
The house must be aired.
Take the child out for an airing.
She puts on too many airs.
I like to build air-castles.
What is our National air?
I bought an air-cushion.
Do you know what an air-thermometer is?
The box must be air-tight.
Have you ever seen an air-pump?
Go out into the fresh air.
Have the house aired before they arrive.
Try to be out in the fresh air as much as possible.
She puts on too many airs.
They have gone out for an airing.
She left the room airily.
Has America a National Air?
How much did you pay for that air-cushion?
Do you believe that airships will ever cross the Atlantic?

An air-thermometer is a thermometer in which air is used instead of mercury.

The air-pump was invented about 1654.

The tea was packed in air-tight chests.

Do you build air-castles?

The band played many of the National airs.

The nurse took the baby out for an airing.

If you spend your time building air-castles you will not accomplish much.

Put the Japanese air-plant in the window.

Take an air-cushion with you if you are going to sit on the rocks.

Let us contribute to the Fresh Air Fund.

She knew many popular airs by heart.

Do you believe that airships will become useful as mail-carriers?

A. Subject

LOOK

B. Word Development

look	onlooker
looks	outlook
looked	lookout
looking	overlook
looking-glass	

C. Conversational Practice

Look it over.
It looks well.
How do you like the looks of it?
What is the outlook?
Look out!
I have been looking for you.
That is a good looking-glass.
I must have overlooked it.
I look forward to seeing her.
Did you look it up?
Look out, you will fall.
I looked for the book but could not find it.
Let me look at your book a moment.
I don't like his looks very well.
It looked like rain when we started.
In looking over some papers, I found this letter.
He did not take part in the play, he was merely an onlooker.
They kept a sharp lookout from the tower.
Have you read "Through the Looking-Glass?"
That is like looking fot a needle in a haystack.

Have you seen the last number of the Outlook?
We must have overlooked the name when we went over the list.
My windows look toward the ocean.
The house looks upon the street.
Will you look after my flowers while I am away?
I look forward to my trip with pleasure.
Let us look into the matter carefully.
I shall look to you for help.
Look up the word in the dictionary.
We were much discouraged over the outlook.
You must look at things from the cheerful side.

A. Subject

WOOD

B. Word Development

wood	woodcraft
wooden	woodcut
woody	wood-engraving
woodbine	woodland
wood-carver	woodpecker
wood-carving	woodpile
wood-chopper	woodwork
woodchuck	woodenware

C. Conversational Practice

Chop the wood.
What kind of wood is that?
The woodbine covers the window.
Did the wood-carver make the frame?
Have you ever tried wood-carving?
Give the axe to the wood-chopper.
See the woodchuck.
Show me the woodcut.
Listen to the woodpecker.
My umbrella has a wooden handle.
You must have all the woodwork painted.
He bought several acres of woodland.
The peddler sold woodenware.
The axe is on the woodpile.
What is the price of a cord of wood?
We have hard wood floors in our new house.
The knife has a plain wooden handle.
The arbor was covered with woodbine.

That man is a skillful wood-carver.

Many people in Switzerland are engaged in the art of wood-carving.

Do you know the story about Daniel Webster and the woodchuck?

I bought a pretty woodcut.

Have you ever seen a red-headed woodpecker?

Be careful not to scratch the woodwork when you move the furniture.

That is a woody tract of land.

There is a large woodpile behind the house.

The fire spread rapidly because the houses were built of wood.

Give the money to the man with the wooden leg.

The wood-chopper returned to his hut before dark.

How many cords of wood are there in that wood-pile?

Buy your furniture to match your woodwork.

The woody land was impossible to cultivate.

The woodenware was not expensive.

Do you think a wooden handle would break?

A. Subject

CROSS

B. Word Development

cross
Maltese Cross
cross-barred
cross-examination
cross-eye
crossing
cross-purposes
cross-questions
cross-road
cross-section
cross-stitch
crosswise
across
crossed
cross lots
grade crossing
cross-legged

C. Conversational Practice

Do not get cross.
Can you draw a Maltese Cross?
The curtains were made of cross-barred muslin.
Who was present at the cross-examination?
Can cross-eye be cured?
Cross-question him.
Let us meet at the cross-road.
Do it in cross-stitch.
Lay the paper cross-wise.
Jump across.
We crossed the brook.
Let us run cross lots.
Stop at the grade crossing.
Do not sit cross-legged.
The cross is the symbol of the Christian faith.
A Maltese cross has eight points.
He was as cross as two sticks when he heard about it.

Please buy me two yards of cross-barred muslin.
He was put through a very thorough cross-examination.
Fold the cloth cross-wise.
The witness broke down under the cross-examination.
They are pursuing cross-purposes.
He was cross-questioned by the officer.
The village postoffice is at the cross-road.
The badge of the Red Cross is a red cross on a white field and the flag of Switzerland is a white cross on a red field.
Who lives in the house across the way?
The idea crossed my mind this morning.
Let us cross lots to the postoffice.
Did you ever see an iceberg while crossing the Atlantic?
In Oriental countries it is the custom for the people to sit cross-legged.
He spoke crossly to the children.
Draw a cross-section of the flower.
The sofa-pillow was embroidered in cross-stitch.
The accident happened when the train reached the crossing.

A. Subject

LIGHT

B. Word Development

light
lighter
lighten
light-footed
footlights
light-hearted
lighthouse
lightly
lightning
lightning-rod
light-minded
light-ship
electric light
gaslight
Bengal light
lightkeeper
light reading
sunlight
moonlight
starlight

C. Conversational Practice

Light the lamp.
Turn on the light.
This is lighter than the other.
How is the house lighted?
Did you ever visit a lighthouse?
Step lightly.
Which do you prefer, electric light or gaslight?
I like sunlight in my room.
Have you ever seen the ocean by moonlight?
What is a light-ship?
Are you afraid of lightning?
There is no light in the room.
I want a lighter shade of blue.
Did you see it lighten just now.
Light the gas.
The deer is light-footed.

How is your new house to be lighted?
He belongs to a regiment of light-infantry.
The lightning continued all through the night.
Have you a lightning-rod on your house?
It was a rule in the school that all lights must be out by ten o'clock.
We passed Nantucket light-ship at four o'clock.
I prefer to read by lamplight.
They used Bengal lights at the festival.
The lightkeeper will be delighted to show you the lighthouse.
Can you recommend something interesting for light reading during the summer?
The lightkeeper led a lonely life.
The strong sunlight will fade the wall paper.
The wind blew out the gas light.
The moonlight filled the room.
Electric light is more powerful than the old-fashioned lamplight.

A. Subject

HIGH

B. Word Development

high	higher	high-priest
high-aimed	highest	high-principled
high-church		highroad
high-heeled		high school
highland		high-sea
highlander		high-sounding
highly		high-treason
high mass		high-water
highness		high-water mark
high-priced		highway.

C. Conversational Practice

How high can you reach?
Her principles were high-aimed
Do you belong to the High Church?
Put on your high-heeled shoes.
We appreciate your kindness highly.
There is high mass at ten o'clock.
That is too high-priced for my purse.
They met on the highroad.
He died on the high-sea.
Did you go through high school?
What a high-sounding name!
Who saw the highwayman?
How high is Mt. Washington?
What is the highest mountain-peak in America?
Are you a member of the High Church?
It is the fashion now to wear high-heeled shoes.

The highlands of Scotland are beautiful.
Did you speak to the highlander?
Her generosity was highly appreciated.
We attended high mass at St. Peter's Church in Rome.
Have you seen Her Royal Highness, the Queen of Holland?
Is that a high-priced book?
She graduated from the high school last year.
There were many high-sounding names on the list.
He was found guilty of high treason.
Show me the high-water mark.
What time is high-water today?
There was an exhibition of drawings at the high school.
The stage-coach was stopped by highway robbers.
The picture was too highly colored.
The new styles are high-priced.
The aviator went higher and higher.

A. Subject

SEA

B. Word Development

sea	seaport
sea-air	sea-salt
sea-breeze	sea-serpent
sea-captain	seashore
sea-coast	seasick
seafarer	seaside
sea-grass	sea-voyage
sea-green	sea-water
sea-gull	seaweed
sea-lion	seaworthy
seaman	sea-shell
sea-mile	sea-urchin

C. Conversational Practice

The sea is calm today.
The sea-air will do you good.
Her father was a sea-captain.
I have a new sea-green gown.
Were you ever seasick?
We spent the summer at the seaside.
We found some pretty sea-shells.
Philadelphia is a seaport.
How long is a sea-mile?
Watch the sea-gulls!
We often sailed along the sea-coast.
Did you ever find a sea-urchin?
We hope the sea-air will do the children good.
The boys like to listen to the stories of the old sea-captain

Her new sea green gown is very becoming.
Hundreds of sea-gulls followed our ship.
Most stories of the sea-serpent and the sea-monster are obviously mythical.
The children had a fine time at the seaside hunting for sea-shells and sea-urchins.
They played among the seaweed and bathed in the sea-water.
They did not enjoy the sail along the sea-coast, however, for the water was rough and they were seasick.
An old seafarer told them a story about a sea-lion.
A long sea-voyage is very restful.
Do you think that old ship is seaworthy?
Can you name five seaports of America?
Do you prefer to spend the summer at the seashore or in the mountains?
We enjoyed our sea-voyage very much.
The old seafarer brought home many rare sea-shells.
Is the sea-mile longer than the geographical mile?
We spent the day at the seashore.
The sea-coast of Maine is deeply indented.
There is much sea-grass on the shore.
Shall we go for a sail along the sea-coast?

A. Subject

LIFE

B. Word Development

life
life-annuity
life-boat
life-buoy
life-estate
life-insurance
life-interest
lifeless
lifelike
lifeline
lifelong
life-preserver
life-rent
lifetime
life-saving station
life-size

C. Conversational Practice

The speaker was full of life.
They were lifelong friends.
Throw out the lifeline.
Put on the life-preserver.
See the life-buoy!
The statue was lifelike.
We visited the life-saving station.
It would take a lifetime to do that.
Life-insurance is a good thing.
The portrait was life-size.
What a useless life they lead.
The captain ordered the life-boats to be lowered.
The man took out a life-insurance policy.
He was a lifelong friend of our family.
Be sure to see the life-saving station.
He spent a lifetime in writing his works.
The blind man was given a life-annuity.

There were not enough life-preservers to go around.
What a lifelike portrait that is!
She has a life-interest in the business.
The life-boat carried twenty people.
The history was the work of a lifetime.
The life-guard hastened to the rescue.
Pay your life-insurance at the office.
"Life is real, life is earnest."
The lifeless form was found on the beach.
His life-annuity was small but adequate.
Every passenger was provided with a life-preserver.
We marvelled at the lifelike portrait of our friend.
We watched the crew leave the life-saving station.

A. Subject

LAND

B. Word Development

land
landed
native land
landing-place
landlady
landlord
landmark
landscape
landscape-gardening
land-slide
island
Highland
lowland
overland
inland

C. Conversational Practice

Who owns this land?
Where did you land?
They landed last night.
What is your native land?
Have you been down to the landing-place?
What is your landlady's name?
That man is our landlord.
What a beautiful landscape!
How large is the island?
Where is Highland Avenue?
Did you go to California by the Overland route?
They live in a small inland town.
We own fifty acres of land.
How much land does your father own?
America is my native land.
Norway is called the "Land of the Midnight Sun."
He has just returned from a visit to the Holy Land.
We landed at Liverpool on the 4th of May.

Let us go down to the landing-place and wait for the boat.
Ask the landlady if we may have the room.
The Washington Elm is one of the old landmarks of Cambridge.
Did you speak to the landlord about the repairs?
Who painted that beautiful landscape?
The boy is interested in landscape-gardening.
Many houses were destroyed by the landslide.
There are many islands in the harbor of Portland.
Have you travelled through the Highlands of Scotland?
There is a dance called the Highland Fling.
We took the Overland route to California.
The landlady had prepared a good meal for the travellers.
"Sweet Land of Liberty" they sang.
The boat reached the landing-place at noon.

A. Subject

PASS

B. Word Development

pass	passe-partout
pass-book	passing
passer-by	Passover
passementerie	passport
passenger	password
passenger-ship	passage
passenger-train	passably

C. Conversational Practice

Pass me the book.
Did you see them pass by?
How many passengers were on the ship?
How much passementerie did you buy?
Is that a passenger-ship or a freight-ship?
She forgot the password.
Did you engage your passage?
The passenger-train was late.
We had a rough passage.
Can you passe-partout the picture for me?
Have you a passport?
I would pass it over.
How shall we pass the time from now until five o'clock?
The clerk made an entry in the pass-book.
We watched the passers-by from the window.
My new dress is to be trimmed with passementerie.
There were several hundred passengers on the ship.
There are several lines of passenger-ships between New York and Europe.

How much will it cost to passe-partout this picture?
She always stops a moment when passing by.
You will need a passport when you travel in Russia.
He forgot the password and was not allowed to enter.
We had a rough passage homeward.
The best thing to do will be to pass it over.
Did you pass in your examinations?
The play was only passably good.
The Passover is an annual feast of the Jews.
Pass the word along.
The shipwrecked sailors hailed a passing steamer.
Send to Washington for your passport.
Let us ask the first passer-by.
The robbers held up the passenger-train.

A. Subject

HEAD

B. Word Development

head	head master
headed	headquarters
heading	head-servant
beheaded	headshake
headlong	headstone
headache	headstrong
head-dress	headway
headless	head-line

C. Conversational Practice

Try to head him off.
You are headed the wrong way.
I read only the heading.
Who is at the head of the class?
My brother is head master in that school.
Who is head-servant at the inn?
I have a headache.
Where are their headquarters?
You are too headstrong.
How much headway did you make?
Don't lose your head.
He fell headlong down the stairs.
There are over 5000 head of cattle on that ranch.
You are headed the wrong way.
King Charles I of England was beheaded.
John is always at the head of his class.
The child fell headlong down the stairs.
He is head and shoulders above the other boys.

You have hit the nail on the head.
We had a head wind and rough sea most of the time.
I shall ask him to head the subscription list.
I don't want to go because I have a headache.
In the 15th Century the style of ladies' head-dress was very elaborate.
I read only the head-lines in the newspaper this morning.
He hopes to become head master of the boys' high school.
We made New York our headquarters for the time being.
She replied by a mere headshake.
A simple headstone was placed on the grave.
She applied for a position as head-servant.
We do not seem to make much headway.
The ship did not make much headway in the storm.
Her odd head-dress was very conspicuous.

A. Subject

SUN

B. Word Development

sun	sunfish
sunbeam	sunflower
sunbird	sunlight
sunburn	sunny
sunburnt	sunproof
Sunday	sunrise
sundial	sunset
sundown	sunshine
sunbonnet	sunshade
sundry	sunstroke

C. Conversational Practice

I hope the sun will shine.
See the sunbeam!
How sunburned you are!
Can you come on Sunday?
Meet me at sundown.
Put the sundries on the bill.
See the sunfish!
Pick a sunflower.
Wait for a sunny day.
That color is sunproof.
Get up at sunrise.
Leave before sunset.
It is very warm in the sun today.
She comes to see me the first Sunday in every month.
Sundry articles were lost.
We have sunflowers in our garden.

You will get sunburnt at the beach.
Stand in the sunlight.
I like plenty of sunshine in my room.
Do you think that shade of blue is sunproof?
She gets up before sunrise every morning.
He had a sunstroke last summer.
Let us take a walk at sundown.
She has a large sunny room on the second floor.
Did you ever see a sundial?
There was a beautiful sunset last evening.
Take your sunshade when you go for a walk.
The farmer's wife wore a sunbonnet.
We must start before sunrise tomorrow.
I hope the sun will shine on Sunday.
If you wear a sunbonnet you will not need a sunshade.
She worked from sunrise to sunset.

A. Subject

HOUSE

B. Word Development

house	
house-boat	housemaid
House of Commons	housewife
House of Representatives	house-warming
house-fly	house-lot
houseful	house-rent
household	house-physician
housekeeping	
housekeeper	

C. Conversational Practice

Who built this house?
My house is too large.
Would you like to live in a house-boat?
Her father is a member of the House of Representatives.
We have a new housemaid.
Do you keep house?
Who is housekeeper in your home?
How much is the house-rent?
Do you like to do housework?
Where is your new house-lot?
She is a good housekeeper.
Who owns the large white house on the hill?
The British Parliament is divided into the House of Lords and the House of Commons.
I would rather keep house than board.
People who live in glass houses must not throw stones.

We always have a houseful of company at Thanksgiving.
The house-fly is a great nuisance.
I must attend to my household duties before I go.
Do you take the "Good Housekeeping Magazine"?
I have just engaged a new housekeeper and a new housemaid.
Her mother was a very thrifty housewife.
They invited us to their house-warming party last week.
My brother bought a house-lot in the suburbs.
House-rent is very high in the city.
The little girl likes to help her mother with the housework.
In China many people live in house-boats.
He has been appointed house-physician in the Children's Hospital.
The whole household was aroused by the cry.
We built a bungalow on our new house-lot.
Pay your house-rent on the first day of the month.
They suspected the housemaid of dishonesty.

A. Subject

PAPER

B. Word Development

paper	transfer-paper
paper (verb)	wrapping-paper
carbon paper	note-paper
India paper	paper money
tarred paper	paper-cutter
newspaper	paper-hanger
oiled paper	paper-mill
tissue-paper	paper-weight

C. Conversational Practice

Have you read the paper?
Please buy me some tissue-paper.
What color tissue-paper do you want?
Have you some heavy wrapping-paper?
I bought a quire of note-paper.
Have you a paper-cutter?
Put the paper-weight on the desk.
Will you have the room papered?
What is carbon paper?
What is transfer paper?
The book has a paper cover.
Have you ever been in a paper mill?
This paper is too thin.
How will you have your room papered?
The walls of the hut were covered with tarred paper.
I would like to have that statement on paper.
Have you read the newspaper this morning?

The book was printed on India paper and bound in soft limp leather.

The booths at the fair were decorated with tissue-paper.

This wrapping-paper is not heavy enough.

How do you like my new note-paper?

In Europe paper money is not so common as in the United States.

She sent me a pretty ivory paper-cutter as a birthday gift.

Paper-hangers and painters are at work in our house this week.

There is a large paper-mill in our town.

Use this stone for a paper-weight.

Please buy me some blue and white tissue paper.

Buy several sheets of wrapping paper.

He is the editor of the newspaper.

You can buy note-paper by the pound or by the box.

Have you selected the wall-paper for your room?

A. Subject

DOOR

B. Word Development

door
folding door
door-bell
doorkeeper
door-knob
door-mat
door-plate
door-step
doorway

C. Conversational Practice

Go to the door.
Who lives next door?
Let them remain out of doors.
Who answered the door-bell?
Ring the door-bell.
The house has a pretty doorway.
Don't stand on the door-step.
My name is on the door-plate.
Who is the doorkeeper?
Close the folding door.
Turn the door-knob.
Wipe your feet on the door-mat.
The front door was open.
The rooms were connected by a folding door.
We rang the door-bell, but no one answered.
The doorkeeper would not allow him to enter.
The child could not reach the door-knob.
She polished the door-plate.
Don't forget to wipe your feet on the door-mat.
She was standing on the door-step when we arrived.

There are some beautiful doorways in Salem.
Is your name on the door-plate?
Do you know the people who live next door?
Ask the doorkeeper for the key.
We waited in the doorway for the rain to cease.
Turn the door-knob and the door will open.
The name was plainly seen on the door-plate.
Stand on the door-step and wait for the car.
She stood in the doorway.
Leave the orders at the side door.
The door-bell is out of order.
The doorkeeper will deliver the letter.

V. Subject

HORSE

B. Word Development

horse
horseback
horse-car
horse-chestnut
horse-dealer
horse-show
horsehair
horseman
horse-race
horse-radish
horse-rake
horseshoe
horseshoe-crab
horse-thief
horsewhip
horsewoman
horse-power

C. Conversational Practice

How many horses do you keep?
Do you ride horseback?
Do you remember when we had horse-cars?
The horse-chestnuts are in bloom.
That man is a horse-dealer.
Did you go to the horse-show?
Who won the horse-race?
Do you like horse-radish?
I found a horseshoe.
Did they catch the horse-thief?
Are you a good horsewoman?
Give me the horsewhip.
That horse belongs to my father.
I would rather ride horseback than play golf.
The day of the horse-car is gone forever.
Horsehair makes a durable cover for furniture.
Can you tell me who won the horse-race yesterday?

Would you like some horse-radish with your oysters?
They use a horse-rake on the farm.
We found a horseshoe on the road to the village.
They overtook the horse-thief on a motorcycle.
I met many of my friends at the horse-show.
She is a very fine horsewoman.
The horse-chestnut tree in front of our house is now in bloom.
Did you ever find a horseshoe-crab?
The horse-dealer rarely gets the worse in a bargain.
The horse-show was opened October first.
The blacksmith will give you a horseshoe.
That horse is a good trotter.
The judge pronounced the horse-thief guilty.
Did the dealer refuse to sell the horse?
Put the horsehair furniture in the large room.

A. Subject

POST

B. Word Development

post	postmaster
posted	postmaster-general
postage	post-mortem
postage-stamp	post-office
postal card	post-paid
post-bag	postpone
poster	postponement
post-horn	postscript
postman	postgraduate
postmark	post-haste

C. Conversational Practice

Post the letter.
Have you a postage-stamp?
Where is the postman?
Go to the post-office.
See the poster!
Why was the meeting postponed?
Did you add a postscript?
Was the package postpaid?
Ask the postmaster about it.
Are you a postgraduate?
Write me a postal card.
How much is the postage?
The wind blew down the telegraph post.
The news was posted on the bulletin-board.
He is well posted in history.
The bookkeeper made a mistake in posting the ledger.

Have you posted my letter?

Can you tell me how much the postage will be on that package?

Send me a postal card when you arrive.

The new theatre posters attracted much attention.

They sent for the doctor post-haste.

The postman left several letters for you this morning.

The postmark was so blurred we could not make out the name.

Whom did they appoint as postmaster?

It would be better to enclose postage-stamps than cash in your letter.

Who is postmaster-general?

They are planning to change the site of our post-office.

The meeting was postponed until next week.

They say the most important part of a woman's letter is the postscript.

The doctors decided to make a post-mortem examination.

He forgot to take the post-bag with him.

He is taking a postgraduate course at Harvard.

A. Subject

LETTER

B. Word Development

letter	letter-carrier
capital letter	letter-file
dead-letter office	letter-head
initial letter	letter-paper
letter of credit	letter-press
registered letter	letter-wood
man of letters	letter-writer
open letter	red-letter day
letter-box	letters of the alphabet

C. Conversational Practice

How many letters did you receive?
Is that word spelled with a capital letter?
Where is the dead-letter office?
Did you receive a registered letter?
Has the letter-carrier been here this morning?
Will you lend me a sheet of letter-paper?
Have you a letter-file?
There is a letter-press in the office.
Have you ever seen letter-wood?
Can you repeat the letters of the alphabet in French?
He was a man of letters.
Please put this letter in the letter-box for me.
The letter must be mailed before noon.
Begin each line with a captal letter.
All unclaimed letters are sent to the dead-letter office.
The initial letters in some of the old books were very ornamental.

I think the Travellers' Checks are a more convenient way of carrying money than a letter of credit.

She received a registered letter from abroad this morning.

An open letter to the president was published in the paper last evening.

There is a letter-box at the corner of the street.

Christmas is a hard time for the letter-carrier.

You will find both a letter-file and a letter-press in the office.

Will you buy me a ream of letter-paper when you go out?

A kind of wood called letter-wood comes from South America.

It was a red-letter day for the children when they went to the circus.

The child learned the letters of the alphabet before he went to school.

Send the letter off at once.

Deliver the letter to the secretary at once.

A. Subject

FIRE

B. Word Development

fire
fiery
firearms
fire-balloon
fire-cracker
fire-engine
fire-escape
firefly
fire-insurance
fire-alarm
fire-irons
fireless
fireman
fireplace
fire-proof
fireweed
fire-wood
fire-works

C. Conversational Practice

Did you see the fire?
They must not play with firearms.
See the fire-balloon!
I burned myself with a fire-cracker.
The fire-engine just passed the house.
Where is the fire-escape?
I like to sit by the fireplace.
Is this building fire-proof?
Do you like to see fireworks?
Watch the fireflies.
Do you know how to build a fire?
There was a fire on our street last night.
The sparks from the engine set the grass on fire.
She has too many irons in the fire.
It is dangerous to carry firearms.
On Fourth of July we saw some fire-balloons.
I heard the fire-engine pass the house early this morning.

The fire-escape is on the other side of the building.
The children caught the fireflies and put them into glass jars.
Be sure to have your fire-insurance policy renewed promptly.
The fire-irons were made of brass.
Do you use a fireless cooker?
One of the firemen was hurt last night.
We have a large open fire-place in out sitting-room.
There was a fine display of fireworks in the park last night.
They have put a new fire-proof safe in the office.
The field was full of fireweed.
The accident was caused by fire-crackers.
Put the papers in a fire-proof safe.
That building has no fire-escape.
The fireman was rewarded for his bravery.

A. Subject

BOOK

B. Word Development

book	
booked	note-book
bookbindery	book-making
bookshelf	book-mark
bookcase	book-plate
booking-office	book-rack
bookkeeper	bookseller
book-knowledge	book-shop
booklet	book-stall
cash-book	book-worm

C. Conversational Practice

Where is my book?
How many books are on the bookshelf?
I bought a bookcase.
The book-rack is made of brass.
Where is the note-book?
Buy a note-book.
Do not lose the book-mark.
Have you a book-plate?
Go to the book-shop with me.
Show me the way to the booking office.
Who is the bookkeeper?
Are you a book-worm?
What is the title of the new book?
We are booked to sail from New York on the third of May.
How much did the bookbinder charge you to rebind the book?

There is a large bookbindery and printing-office on State street.

Place the book on the bookshelf in the library.

Meet me at the booking office of the Steamship Company at four o'clock.

Her brother is bookkeeper for a large firm.

They have not much book-knowledge.

At Christmas time there are many pretty booklets on sale.

Please lend me your note-book.

Who discovered the art of book-making?

Use this card for a book-mark.

My brother has an interesting collection of book-plates.

The boys carved some book-racks.

Ask the bookseller to send me the latest novel.

There is a large book-shop at the corner of our street.

Who will have charge of the book-stall at the fair?

That bookcase will be too large for my room.

The family declared the child was too much of a book-worm.

The bookkeeper could not find the mistake in the cash-book.

Printed in the United Kingdom
by Lightning Source UK Ltd.
114918UKS00001B/70